D0457815

NOTES ON THE
DEATH OF CULTURE

NOTES ON THE DEATH OF CULTURE

Essays on Spectacle and Society

MARIO VARGAS LLOSA

EDITED AND TRANSLATED FROM
THE SPANISH BY JOHN KING

FARRAR, STRAUS AND GIROUX

NEW YORK

Farrar, Straus and Giroux
18 West 18th Street, New York 10011

Library of Congress Cataloging-in-Publication Data
Vargas Llosa, Mario, 1936– author.
  [Civilización del espectáculo. English]
  Notes on the death of culture : essays on spectacle and society / Mario
Vargas Llosa ; edited and translated from the Spanish by John King.
    pages   cm
  ISBN 978-0-374-12304-8 (hardback) — ISBN 978-0-374-71031-6 (e-book)
  1. Civilization, Modern—20th century—Philosophy.   2. Culture—
Philosophy—20th century.   3. Social problems—History—20th century.
I. King, John, 1950– translator.   II. Title.

CB428 .V3713 2015
909.82—dc23

                                                        2014049063

Farrar, Straus and Giroux books may be purchased for educational,
business, or promotional use. For information on bulk purchases,
please contact the Macmillan Corporate and Premium Sales
Department at 1-800-221-7945, extension 5442, or write to
specialmarkets@macmillan.com.

www.fsgbooks.com
www.twitter.com/fsgbooks • www.facebook.com/fsgbooks

1   3   5   7   9   10   8   6   4   2

For Juan Cruz Ruiz,
always with his notebook and pencil

The hours have lost their clock.
VICENTE HUIDOBRO

Contents

NOTES ON THE
DEATH OF CULTURE

Metamorphosis of a Word

It is very likely that never in human history have there been as many treatises, essays, theories and analyses focused on culture as there are today. This fact is even more surprising given that culture, in the meaning traditionally ascribed to the term, is now on the point of disappearing. And perhaps it has already disappeared, discreetly emptied of its content, and replaced by another content that distorts its earlier meaning.

This short essay does not intend to add to the large number of interpretations of contemporary culture but rather to explore the metamorphosis of what was still understood as culture when my generation was in school or at university, and the motley definitions that have replaced it, an adulteration that seems to have come about quite easily, without much resistance.

Before developing my own argument, I would like to explore, albeit in summary fashion, some of the essays that, in recent decades, have focused on this topic from different perspectives, and have at times stimulated important intellectual and political debates. Although they are very different from each other, and are only a small sample of the ideas and theses that the subject has inspired, they do share a common denominator in so far as they all agree that culture is in deep crisis and is in decline. The final analysis in this chapter, by contrast, talks of a new culture built on the ruins of what it has come to replace.

I begin this review with the famous, and polemical, declaration by T. S. Eliot. Although it is only some sixty-seven years since he published, in 1948, his essay *Notes Towards the Definition of Culture*, when we reread it today, it seems to refer to a very remote era, without any connection to the present.

T. S. Eliot assures us that his aim is merely to help define the concept of culture, but, in fact, his ambition is much greater, for, as well as specifying what the term means, he offers a penetrating criticism of the cultural system of his time, which, according to him, is becoming ever more distant from the ideal model that it represented in the past. In a sentence that might have appeared excessive at the time of writing, he argues, 'I see no reason why the decay of culture should not proceed much further, and why we may not even anticipate a period, of some duration, of which it will be possible to say that it will have *no* culture.'[1] (Anticipating my argument in *Notes on the Death of Culture*, I will say that the period Eliot is referring to is the one in which we are now living.)

That ideal older model, according to Eliot, is a culture made up of three 'senses' of the term: the individual, the group or class, and the whole society. While there is some interaction between these three areas, each maintains a

1 T. S. Eliot, *Notes Towards the Definition of Culture*, paperback edition, Faber & Faber, London, 1962, p. 19.

certain autonomy and develops in a state of constant tension with the others, within an order that allows the whole of society to prosper and maintain its cohesiveness.

T. S. Eliot states that what he calls 'higher culture' is the domain of an elite, and he justifies this by asserting that 'it is an essential condition of the preservation of the quality of the culture of a minority, that it should continue to be a minority culture' (p. 107). Like the elite, social class is also a reality that must be maintained, because the caste or group that guarantees higher culture is drawn from these ranks, an elite that should not be completely identified with the privileged group or aristocracy from which most of its members are drawn. Each class has the culture that it produces and that is appropriate to it and although, naturally, these cultures coexist, there are also marked differences that have to do with the economic conditions of each. One cannot conceive of an identical aristocratic and rural culture, for example, even though both classes share many things, such as religion and language.

Eliot's idea of class is not rigid or impermeable; rather it is open. A person from one class can move up or down a class, and it is good that this happens, even though it is an exception rather than the rule. This system both guarantees and expresses a social order, but today this order is fractured, which creates uncertainty about the future. The naive idea that, through education, one can transmit culture to all of society is destroying 'higher culture', because the only way of achieving this universal democratization of culture is by impoverishing culture, making it ever more superficial. Just as the elite is indispensable to Eliot's conception of 'higher culture', so also it is fundamental that a society has regional cultures that both nurture national culture and also exist in their own right with a certain degree of independence. 'It is important that a man should feel himself to be not merely a citizen of a particular nation, but a citizen of a particular part of his country, with local loyalties. These, like loyalty to class, arise out of loyalty to the family' (p. 52).

Culture is transmitted through the family and when this institution ceases to function in an adequate way, the result is that 'we must expect our culture to deteriorate' (p. 43). Outside the family the main form of transmission of culture through the generations has been the Church, not the school. We should not confuse culture with knowledge. 'Culture is not merely the sum of several activities, but *a way of life*' (p. 41), a way of life where forms are as important as content. Knowledge is concerned with the evolution of technology and the sciences, and culture is something that predates knowledge, an attribute of the spirit, a sensibility and a cultivation of form that gives sense and direction to different spheres of knowledge.

Culture and religion are not the same thing, but they are not separable because culture was born within religion and even though, with the historical evolution of humanity, it has partially drawn away from religion, it will always be connected to its source of nourishment by a sort of umbilical cord. Religion, 'while it lasts, and on its own level, gives an apparent meaning to life, provides the framework for a culture and protects the mass of humanity from boredom and despair' (p. 34).

When he speaks of religion, T. S. Eliot is referring fundamentally to Christianity, which, he says, has made Europe what it is:

It is in Christianity that our arts have developed; it is in Christianity that the laws of Europe have – until recently – been rooted. It is against a background of Christianity that all our thought has significance. An individual European may not believe that the Christian Faith is true, and yet what he says, and makes, and does, will all spring out of his heritage of Christian culture and depend on that culture for its meaning. Only a Christian culture could have produced a Voltaire or a Nietzsche. I do not believe that the culture of Europe could survive the complete disappearance of the Christian Faith. (p. 122)

Eliot's idea of society and culture brings to mind the structure of heaven, purgatory and hell in Dante's *Commedia* with its superimposed circles and its rigid symmetries and hierarchies in which the divinity punishes evil and rewards good according to an intangible order.

Some twenty years after Eliot's book was published, George Steiner replied to it, in 1971, in his *In Bluebeard's Castle: Some Notes Towards the Re-definition of Culture*. In his concise and intense essay, Steiner is disturbed that the great poet of *The Waste Land* could have written a treatise on culture just three years after the end of the Second World War without linking his discussion in any way to the extraordinary carnage of the two world wars, and, above all, without mentioning the Holocaust, the extermination of 6 million Jews, the culmination of a long tradition of anti-Semitism within Western culture. Steiner proposes to remedy this defect with an analysis of culture that gives primacy to its association with political and social violence.

In Steiner's account, after the French Revolution, Napoleon, the Napoleonic wars, the Bourbon Restoration and the triumph of the bourgeoisie in Europe, the Old Continent fell prey to 'the great *ennui*', a sense of frustration, tedium and melancholy, mixed in with a secret desire for explosive, cataclysmic violence, which can be found in the best European literature and in works such as Freud's *Civilization and Its Discontents*. The Dada and surrealist movements were at the cutting edge and the most acute forms of this phenomenon. For Steiner, European culture did not simply anticipate but it also desired the prospect of a bloody and purging explosion that took shape in revolutions and in two world wars. Instead of stopping these bloodbaths, culture desired to provoke and celebrate them.

Steiner insinuates that perhaps the reason why Eliot had not encompassed 'the phenomenology of mass murder as it took place in Europe, from the Spanish south to the frontiers of Russian Asia between 1936 and 1945,'[2] was his anti-Semitism, private at first, but which the publication of

---

2 George Steiner, *In Bluebeard's Castle: Some Notes Towards the Redefinition of Culture*, Faber & Faber, London, 1971, p. 34.

some of his correspondence, after his death, would bring to public attention. His case is not exceptional because 'there have been few attempts to relate the dominant phenomenon of twentieth-century barbarism to a more general theory of culture'. And, Steiner adds,

A theory of culture, an analysis of our present circumstance, which do not have at their pivot a consideration of the modes of terror that brought on the death, through war, starvation and deliberate massacre, of some seventy million human beings in Europe and Russia between the start of the First World War and the end of the Second, seem to me irresponsible (pp 31–?)

Steiner's explanation is closely associated with religion, which, in his opinion, is at the core of culture, as Eliot argued, but without Eliot's narrow defence of 'Christian discipline', which is 'now the most vulnerable aspect of his argument' (p. 71). In Steiner's argument, the 'thrust of will' that gives rise to art and to disinterested thought, is 'rooted in a gamble on transcendence' (p. 71). This is the religious aspect of every culture. Western culture has been plagued by anti-Semitism from time immemorial, and the reason for this is religious. It is a vengeful response of the non-Jewish world to a people who invented monotheism, that is, the concept of a unique, invisible, inconceivable and all-powerful god who is beyond human comprehension and imagination. The Mosaic god came to replace the polytheism of gods and goddesses who were accessible to humanity in its different forms, and with whom diverse men and women could feel comfortable and get along. Christianity, for Steiner, with its saints, the mystery of the Trinity and the cult of the Virgin Mary, was always 'a hybrid of monotheistic ideals and polytheistic practices' (p. 37), which thus managed to revive some of the proliferation of divinities abolished by the monotheism of Moses. The unique, inconceivable god of the Jews is outside human reason – it is accessible only through faith – and it fell victim to the *philosophes* of the Enlightenment, who were convinced that a lay, secular culture would put an end to the violence and killings resulting from religious fanaticism, inquisitorial practices and wars of religion. But the death of God did not signify the advent of paradise on earth, but rather a hell, already prefigured in the Dantesque nightmare of the *Commedia* or in the pleasure palaces and torture chambers of the Marquis de Sade. The world, liberated from God, gradually became dominated by the devil, a spirit of evil, cruelty and destruction that would culminate in the world wars, the Nazi crematoriums and the Soviet Gulag. With this cataclysm culture came to an end and the era of post-culture began.

Steiner emphasizes that feelings of 'self-indictment' or remorse are at the heart of the Western tradition: 'What other races have turned in penitence to those whom they once enslaved, what other civilizations have morally indicted the brilliance of their own past? This reflex of self-scrutiny in the name of ethical absolutes is, once more, a characteristically Western, post-Voltairian act' (p. 55).

One of the characteristics of post-culture is not to

8

believe in progress, that history is on an ascendant curve. Instead we find a *Kulturpessimismus* or a new stoic realism (p. 57). Curiously this attitude coexists with evidence that, in the fields of technology and scientific understanding, our era is producing miracles on a daily basis. But modern progress, we now know, often has a price to pay in terms of destruction, for example, with the irreparable damage done to nature and ecological systems, and it does not always serve to decrease poverty but rather to widen the chasm of inequality between countries, classes and peoples.

Post-culture has destroyed the myth that the humanities humanize. What so many optimistic educationalists and philosophers believed, that a liberal education accessible to all would guarantee a future of progress, peace, liberty and equality of opportunity in modern democracies, has not proved to be the case: ' . . . the libraries, museums, theatres, universities, research centres, in and through which the transmission of the humanities and of the sciences mainly takes place, can prosper next to the concentration camps' (p. 63). In individuals, as in society, high culture, sensibility and intelligence can, at times, coexist with the fanaticism of the torturer and the assassin. Heidegger was a Nazi, but he composed his great work on the philosophy of language within earshot of a death camp: 'Heidegger's pen did not stop, nor his mind go mute' (p. 63).

In the stoic pessimism of post-culture, the security that certain differences and hierarchical value structures once offered have now disappeared: 'The line of division separated the higher from the lower, the greater from the lesser; civilization from retarded primitivism, learning from ignorance, social privilege from subservience, seniority from immaturity, men from women. And each time "from" stood also for "above"' (p. 66). The collapse of these distinctions is now the most salient feature of contemporary culture.

Post-culture, which is sometimes also called, significantly, the 'counter-culture', can admonish culture for its elitism and for the traditional links that the arts, literature and science have had with political absolutism: 'What good did high humanism do the oppressed mass of the community? What use was it when barbarism came?' (p. 69)

In his final chapters, Steiner sketches a rather gloomy picture of how culture might evolve, in which tradition, lacking any validity, would be confined to academia: 'Already a dominant proportion of poetry, of religious thought, of art, has receded from personal immediacy into the keeping of the specialist' (p. 83). What was previously active life will become the artificial life of the archive. And, worse still, culture will be the victim – it is already the victim – of what Steiner calls 'the retreat from the word'. Traditionally, 'spoken, remembered and written discourse was the backbone of consciousness' (p. 86). Now the word is increasingly subordinated to the image. And to music, the 'universal dialect' of the new generations, where rock and pop and folk music create an enveloping space, a world in which writing, studying and private communication 'now take place in a field of strident *vibrato*' (p. 90). What effect will this 'musicalization' of our culture have on our brains, our mental faculties?

As well as stressing the progressive decline of the word, Steiner also points out as salient features of our time the preoccupation with nature and ecology and the prodigious development of the sciences – mathematics and natural sciences in the main – which has revealed unexpected aspects of human life, the natural world and atomic and interstellar space, and created techniques capable of altering and manipulating the brains and behaviour of human beings. The 'bookish' culture that Eliot referred to exclusively in his work is losing its vitality and it exists on the margins of contemporary culture, which has cut itself off almost exclusively from classical humanities – Hebrew, Greek and Latin – while the humanities themselves become the refuge of specialists who remain almost inaccessible due to their hermetic jargon, their asphyxiating erudition and their often delirious theories.

The most polemical part of Steiner's essay is where he argues that postmodern society requires all cultured men and women to have a basic knowledge of mathematics and natural science so that they can understand the notable advances that the scientific world has made and continues to make in every area of chemistry, physics and astronomy, that are often as prodigious as the most audacious inventions of fantastic literature. This proposition is as utopian as those that Steiner decries in his essay, because if in the recent past it was unimaginable that a contemporary Pico della Mirandola would be capable of embracing all the knowledge of his time, in our age this would be out of reach even of those computers much admired by Steiner, with their infinite capacity for storing data. It is possible that culture is no longer possible in our age, but not for this reason given by Steiner, because the very idea of culture never implied any given quantity of knowledge, but rather a certain quality and sensitivity. As with Steiner's other essays, this one begins with its feet on the ground and ends in an explosion of wild intellectual speculations.

A few years before Steiner's essay, in November 1967, Guy Debord published in Paris *La Société du spectacle*, whose title is similar to the subtitle of my own collection of essays, although it approaches the theme of culture in different ways. Debord, an autodidact, a radical avant-garde thinker, a militant and a promoter of 1960s counter-cultural events, defines as 'spectacle' what Marx called 'alienation' in his *Economic and Philosophical Manuscripts of 1844*, a condition caused by commodity fetishism, which, in advanced capitalist societies, has taken on such a central role in the life of consumers that it has displaced any other cultural, intellectual or political reality. The obsessive acquisition of manufactured products, which keeps commodity production actively increasing, brings about the 'reification' of individuals, *turns them into objects*. Men and women become active consumers of objects – many of which are useless or superfluous – that fashion and advertising impose on them, emptying them of social, spiritual or even human concerns, isolating them and destroying their consciousness of others, of their class and of themselves to such an extent that, for example, the proletariat, 'deproletarianized' by alienation, is no longer a danger, or even a form of opposition, to the dominant class.

These ideas of the young Marx, which he never managed to develop in his mature writings, are at the basis of Debord's theory of our times. His central thesis is that in modern industrial society, where capitalism has triumphed and the working class has been (at least temporarily) defeated, alienation – the illusion of a lie that has become a truth – has taken over social existence, turning it into a representation in which everything that is spontaneous, authentic and genuine – the truth of humanity – has been replaced by artificiality and falsehood. In this world, things – commodities – have become the real controllers of life, the masters that men and women serve in order to guarantee the production that enriches the owners of the machines and industries that manufacture these commodities. 'The spectacle', Debord says, 'is the effective dictatorship of illusion in modern society.'[3]

Although in other areas Debord takes many liberties with Marxist theories, he accepts as canonical truth the

3 Guy Debord, *La Société du spectacle*, Gallimard, Paris, 1992, proposition 213.

theory of history as class struggle and the 'reification' of men and women as a result of capitalism, which creates artificial needs, fashions and desires in order to maintain an ever-expanding market for manufactured goods. Written in an abstract and impersonal style, his book contains 9 chapters and 221 propositions, some as short as aphorisms, and almost all lacking concrete examples. His arguments are at times difficult to follow given the intricate nature of his writing. Specifically cultural topics, relating to the arts and literature, are given only marginal coverage. His thesis is economic, philosophical and historical rather than cultural, an aspect of life that, faithful to classic Marxism, Debord reduces to a superstructure built on the relations of production that are the foundations of social existence.

This essay, by contrast, is anchored in the realm of culture, understood not as a mere epiphenomenon of social and economic life, but as an autonomous reality, made up of ideas, aesthetic and ethical values, and works of art and literature that interact with the rest of social existence, and that are often not mere reflections, but rather the wellsprings, of social, economic, political and even religious phenomena.

Debord's book has a number of insights and intuitions that coincide with certain topics that are explored in my essay, such as the idea that replacing life by representation, turning life into a spectator of itself, leads to an impoverishment of human existence (proposition 30). Likewise, his assertion that, in an environment in which life is no longer lived, but rather represented, one lives by proxy, like actors who portray their false lives on stage or screen: 'The real consumer becomes a consumer of illusions' (proposition 47). This lucid observation has been amply confirmed in the years following the publication of Debord's book.

This process, Debord states, leads to a sense of futility 'which dominates modern society' due to the multiplication of commodities that the consumer can choose, and the disappearance of freedom because any social or political changes that occur are not due to the free choices of individuals, but rather to 'the economic system, the dynamic of capitalism'.

Far removed from structuralism, which he calls a 'cold dream', Debord adds that any critique of the society of the spectacle will be possible only as part of a 'practical' critique of the conditions that allow it to exist: practical in the sense of instigating revolutionary action that would bring an end to this society (proposition 203). In this respect, above all, his arguments are diametrically opposed to mine.

A large number of studies in recent years have looked to define the characteristics of contemporary culture within the context of the globalization of capitalism and of markets, and the extraordinary revolution in technology. One of the most incisive of these studies is Gilles Lipovetsky and Jean Serroy's *La cultura-mundo: Respuesta a una sociedad desorientada* (*Culture-World: Response to a Disoriented Society*). It puts forward the idea that there is now an established global culture – a culture-world – that, as a result of the progressive erosion of borders due to market forces, and of scientific and technical revolutions (especially in the field of communications), is creating, for the first time in history, certain cultural values that are shared by societies and individuals across the five continents, values that can be shared equally despite different traditions, beliefs and languages. This culture, unlike what had previously been defined as culture, is no longer elitist, erudite and exclusive, but rather a genuine 'mass culture':

Diametrically opposed to hermetic and elitist vanguard movements, this mass culture seeks to offer innovations that are accessible to the widest possible audience, which will entertain the greatest number of consumers. Its intention is to amuse and offer pleasure, to provide an easy and accessible escapism for everyone without the need for any specific educational background, without concrete and erudite references. What the culture industries invent is a culture transformed into articles of mass consumption.[4]

This mass culture, according to the authors, is based on the predominance of image and sound over the word. The film industry, in particular Hollywood, 'globalizes' movies, sending them to every country, and within each country, reaching every social group, because, like commercially available music and television, films are accessible to

4 Gilles Lipovetsky and Jean Serroy, *La cultura-mundo: Respuesta a una sociedad desorientada*, Anagrama, Barcelona, 2010, p. 79.

everyone and require no specialist background to be enjoyed. This process has been accelerated by the cybernetic revolution, the creation of social networks and the universal reach of the Internet. Not only has information broken through all barriers and become accessible to all, but almost every aspect of communication, art, politics, sport, religion, etc., has felt the reforming effects of the small screen: 'The screen world has dislocated, desynchronized and deregulated the space–time of culture' (p. 88).

All this is true, of course. What is not clear is whether what Lipovetsky and Serroy call the 'culture-world' or mass culture (in which they include, for example, even the 'culture of brands' of luxury objects), is, strictly speaking, culture, or if we are referring to essentially different things when we speak, on one hand, about an opera by Wagner or Nietzsche's philosophy and, on the other hand, the films of Alfred Hitchcock and John Ford (two of my favourite directors), and an advertisement for Coca-Cola. They would say yes, that both categories are culture, while I think that there has been a change, or a Hegelian qualitative leap, that has turned this second category into something different from the first. In the two following chapters I shall explain why.

Furthermore, some assertions of *La cultura-mundo* seem questionable, such as the proposition that this new planetary culture has developed extreme individualism across the globe. Quite the reverse: the ways in which advertising and fashion shape and promote cultural products today are a major obstacle to the formation of independent individuals, capable of judging for themselves what they like, what they admire, or what they find disagreeable, deceitful or horrifying in these products. Rather than developing individuals, the culture-world stifles them, depriving them of lucidity and free will, causing them to react to the dominant 'culture' with a conditioned, herd mentality, like Pavlov's dogs reacting to the bell that rings for a meal.

Another of Lipovetsky's and Serroy's ideas that seems questionable is the assertion that because millions of tourists visit the Louvre, the Acropolis and the Greek amphitheatres in Sicily, then culture has lost none of its value, and still enjoys 'a great legitimacy' (p. 118). The authors seem not to notice that these mass visits to great museums and classic historical monuments do not illustrate a genuine interest in 'high culture' (the term they use), but rather simple snobbery because the fact of having been in these places is part of the obligations of the perfect postmodern tourist. Instead of stimulating an interest in the classical past and its arts, these visits replace any form of serious study and investigation. A quick look is enough to satisfy people that their cultural conscience is clear. These tourist visits 'on the lookout for distractions' undermine the real significance of these museums and monuments, putting them on the same level as other obligations of the perfect tourist: eating pasta and dancing a tarantella in Italy, applauding flamenco and *cante jondo* in Andalucía, and tasting *escargots*, visiting the Louvre and the Folies- Bergère in Paris.

In 2010, Flammarion in Paris published *Mainstream* by the sociologist Frédéric Martel. This book demonstrates that, to some extent, the 'new culture' or the 'culture-world' that Lipovetsky and Serroy speak of is already a thing of the past, out of kilter with the frantic maelstrom of our age. Martel's book is fascinating and terrifying in its description of the 'entertainment culture' that has replaced almost everywhere what scarcely half a century ago was understood as culture. *Mainstream* is, in effect, an ambitious study, drawing on hundreds of interviews from many parts of the world, of what, thanks to globalization and the audio-visual revolution, is now shared by people across five continents, despite differences in languages, religions and customs.

Martel's study does not talk about books – the only one mentioned in its several hundred pages is Dan Brown's *The Da Vinci Code*, and the only woman writer mentioned is the film critic Pauline Kael – or about painting and sculpture, or about classical music and dance, or about philosophy or the humanities in general. Instead it talks exclusively about films, television programmes, videogames, manga, rock, pop and rap concerts, videos and tablets and the 'creative industries' that produce and promote them: that is, the entertainment enjoyed by the vast majority of people that has been replacing (and will end up finishing off) the culture of the past.

The author approves of this change, because, as a result,

mainstream culture has swept away the cultural life of a small minority that had previously held a monopoly over culture; it has democratized it, putting it within everyone's reach, and because the contents of this new culture seem to him to be perfectly attuned to modernity, to the great scientific and technological inventions of our era.

The accounts and the interviews collected by Martel, along with his own analysis, are instructive and quite representative of a reality that, until now, sociological and philosophical studies have not dared to address. The great majority of humanity does not engage with, produce or appreciate any form of culture other than what used to be considered by cultured people, disparagingly, as mere popular pastimes, with no links to the intellectual, artistic and literary activities that were once at the heart of culture. This former culture is now dead, although it still survives in small social enclaves, without any influence on the mainstream.

The essential difference between the culture of the past and the entertainment of today is that the products of the former sought to transcend mere present time, to endure, to stay alive for future generations, while the products of the latter are made to be consumed instantly and disappear, like cake or popcorn. Tolstoy, Thomas Mann, still more Joyce and Faulkner, wrote books that looked to defeat death, outlive their authors and continue attracting and fascinating readers in the future. Brazilian soaps, Bollywood movies and Shakira concerts do not look to exist any longer than the duration of their performance. They disappear and leave space for other equally successful and ephemeral products. Culture is entertainment and what is not entertaining is not culture.

Martel's investigation shows that this is today a global phenomenon, something that is occurring for the first time in history, in which developed and underdeveloped countries participate, no matter how different their traditions, beliefs or systems of government although, of course, each country and society will display certain differences in terms of detail and nuance with regard to films, soap operas, songs, manga, animation, etc.

What this new culture needs is mass industrial production and commercial success. The difference between price and value has disappeared; they are now the same thing, where price has absorbed and cancelled out value. What is successful and sells is good, and what fails or does not reach the public is bad. The only value is commercial value. The disappearance of the old culture implied the disappearance of the old concept of value. The only existing value is now what the market dictates.

From T. S. Eliot to Frédéric Martel, the idea of culture has witnessed much more than a gradual evolution: instead it has seen a traumatic change, in which a new reality has appeared that contains only scant traces of what it has replaced.

I

The Civilization of the Spectacle

Claudio Pérez, a correspondent sent by *El País* to New York to cover the financial crisis, wrote in an article published on Friday, 19 September 2008: 'The New York tabloids are rushing around like madmen looking for a broker about to fling himself into the void from the top of one of those imposing skyscrapers which house the major investment banks, the fallen idols that the financial hurricane has been reducing to rubble.' Let's keep hold of this image for a moment: a pack of photographers, paparazzi, scouring the skyline, cameras at the ready, waiting to capture the first suicide that would be a graphic, dramatic and spectacular embodiment of the financial catastrophe that wiped out billions of dollars and ruined big businesses and countless ordinary people. There can be no better image, I think, that encapsulates our contemporary civilization.

It seems to me that this is the best way to define the civilization of our time, a civilization shared by Western countries, countries in Asia that have achieved high levels of development and many nations in the so-called Third World.

What do we mean by civilization of the spectacle? The civilization of a world in which pride of place, in terms of a scale of values, is given to entertainment, and where having a good time, escaping boredom, is the universal passion. To have this goal in life is perfectly legitimate, of course. Only a Puritan fanatic could reproach members of a society for wanting to find relaxation, fun and amusement in lives that are often circumscribed by depressing and sometimes soul-destroying routine. But converting this natural propensity for enjoying oneself into a supreme value has unexpected consequences: it leads to culture becoming banal, frivolity becoming widespread and, in the field of news coverage, it leads to the spread of irresponsible journalism based on gossip and scandal.

What has caused the West to slide towards this kind of civilization? The material well-being that followed the years of privation during the Second World War and the shortages of the post-war years. After this very tough period, there was a moment of extraordinary economic growth. In every democratic and liberal society in Europe and North America, the middle classes grew exponentially, there was increased social mobility and, at the same time, there was a notable extension of moral parameters, beginning with our sex lives, which had traditionally been held in check by churches and by the prudish secularism of political parties, from right and left. Well-being, a freer lifestyle and the increased time given to leisure in the developed world gave an important stimulus to leisure industries, promoted by advertising, the inspiration and magical guide for our times. So, systematically and imperceptibly, not being bored, avoiding anything that might be disturbing, worrying or distressing, became for increasing numbers both at the pinnacle and at the base of the social pyramid, a generational mandate, what Ortega y Gasset called 'the spirit of our time', a fun, spoiled and frivolous god to which, wittingly or unwittingly, we have been paying increasing allegiance for at least fifty years.

Another, no less important, factor in the shaping of this reality has been the democratization of culture. This is a phenomenon born of altruism: culture could no longer be the patrimony of an elite; liberal and democratic society had a moral obligation to make culture accessible to all, through education and through promoting and supporting the arts, literature and other cultural expression. This commendable philosophy has had the undesired effect of trivializing and cheapening cultural life, justifying superficial form and content in works on the grounds of fulfilling a civic duty to reach the greatest number. Quantity at the expense of quality. This criterion, the domain of the worst demagogues in the political arena, has caused unexpected reverberations in the cultural sphere, such as the disappearance of high culture, by its very nature a minority undertaking due to the complexity and on occasion hermetic nature of its codes, and the massification of the very concept of culture. Culture has now become exclusively accepted in its anthropological definition. That is, culture is all the manifestations of the life of a community: its language, beliefs, habits and customs, clothing, skills and, in short, everything that is exercised, avoided, respected or hated in that community. When the idea of culture becomes an amalgam of this kind, then it is inevitable that it might come to be understood merely as a pleasant way of spending time. Of course, culture can indeed be a pleasing pastime, but if it is just this, then the very concept becomes distorted and debased: everything included under the term becomes equal and uniform; a Verdi opera, the philosophy of Kant, a concert by the Rolling Stones and a performance by the Cirque du Soleil have equal value.

It is not surprising therefore that the most representative literature of our times is 'light', easy literature, which, without any sense of shame, sets out to be – as its primary and almost exclusive objective – entertaining. But let's be clear: I am not in any way condemning the authors of this entertainment literature because, notwithstanding the levity of their texts, they include some really talented writers. If today it is rare to see literary adventures as daring as those of Joyce, Woolf, Rilke or Borges, it is not just down to the writers. For the culture in which we live does not favour, but rather discourages, the indefatigable efforts that produce works that require of the readers an intellectual concentration almost as great as that of their writers. Today's readers require easy books that entertain them and this demand creates a pressure that becomes a powerful incentive to writers.

It is also not accidental that criticism has all but disappeared from the news media and has taken refuge in those cloistered communities called humanities faculties, and in particular in literature departments, whose work is accessible only to specialists. It is true that the more serious newspapers and journals still publish reviews of books, exhibitions and concerts, but does anyone read these solitary paladins who try to map a scale of value onto the tangled jungle that contemporary culture has become? In the days of our grandfathers and great-grandfathers, criticism played a central role in the world of culture because it helped guide citizens in the difficult task of judging what they heard, saw and read. Now critics are a dying breed, to whom nobody pays attention unless they also turn themselves into a form of entertainment and spectacle.

Light literature, along with light cinema and light art, give the reader and the viewer the comfortable impression that they are cultured, revolutionary, modern and in the vanguard without having to make the slightest intellectual effort. Culture that purports to be avant-garde and iconoclastic instead offers conformity in its worst forms: smugness and self-satisfaction.

In the civilization of our times, it is normal, and almost obligatory, for cookery and fashion to take up most of the culture sections, for chefs and fashion designers now enjoy the prominence that before was given to scientists, composers and philosophers. Gas burners, stoves and catwalks meld, in the cultural coordinates of our time, with books, laboratories and operas, while TV stars and great footballers exert the sort of influence over habits, taste and fashion that was previously the domain of teachers and thinkers and (further back still) theologians. Half a century ago in the United States, it was probably Edmund Wilson, in his articles in *The New Yorker* or *The New Republic*, who decided the success or failure of a book, a poem, a novel or an essay. Now the *Oprah Winfrey Show* makes these decisions.

The vacuum left by the disappearance of criticism has been filled, imperceptibly, by advertising, and advertising is now not just an integral part of cultural life, it is its main vector. Advertising plays a decisive role in forming taste, sensibility, imagination and customs. Anonymous 'creative' people in advertising agencies now fulfil the role previously played, in this sphere, by philosophical systems, religious beliefs, ideologies and doctrines and the mentors that in France were called the 'mandarins' of an age. It was perhaps inevitable that this would happen from the moment when artistic and literary works came to be considered as commercial products, whose very survival or extinction depended on the fluctuations of the market, that tragic period in which the *price* became confused with the *value* of a work of art. When a culture relegates critical thinking to the attic of items no longer in fashion and replaces ideas with images, then literary and artistic products are promoted, accepted or rejected through advertising techniques and the conditioned reflexes of a public that lacks the intellectual and discriminatory antennae to detect when it is being duped. By this route, the exaggerated fashions that John Galliano displayed on Parisian catwalks (before it was discovered that he was anti-Semitic), or experiments in nouvelle cuisine, achieve the status of honorary citizens of high culture.

This state of affairs has also led to the celebration of music, to such an extent that it has become a badge of identity for new generations the world over. Fashionable bands and singers attract huge crowds to their concerts, which, like the Dionysian pagan festivals that celebrated irrationality in ancient Greece, are collective ceremonies of excess and catharsis, worshipping instinct, passion and unreason. The same can be said, of course, of the packed electronic music parties, raves, where people dance in the darkness, listen to trance-inducing music and get high on ecstasy. It is not too far-fetched to compare these celebrations to the great religious popular festivals of old. For we find, in secular form, a religious spirit that, in keeping with the spirit of the age, has replaced the liturgy and catechisms of traditional religions with these displays of musical mysticism where, to the rhythm of raw voices and instruments, both amplified to an inaudible level, individuals are no longer individuals; they become a mass, and unwittingly return to the primitive times of magic and the tribe. This is the modern and, of course, much more amusing way of achieving the ecstasy that St Teresa or St John of the Cross found through asceticism, prayer and faith. In these crowded parties and concerts young people today commune, confess, achieve redemption and find fulfilment through this intense, elemental experience of becoming lost to themselves.

Massification, along with frivolity, is another feature of our time. Nowadays sport has acquired an importance matched only in ancient Greece. For Plato, Socrates,

Aristotle and other regular visitors to the Academy, the cultivation of the body was coextensive with and complementary to the cultivation of the spirit, because they believed that both were mutually enriching. The difference with today is that, now, people usually play sports at the expense of, and instead of, intellectual pursuits. In the sporting field football stands out. It is a mass phenomenon that, like modern popular-music concerts, attracts large crowds and raises passions to a greater degree than any other public mobilization, be it political meetings, religious processions or civic assemblies. Of course for the fans – and I am one of them – a football game can be a magnificent spectacle of skill and harmony, with justifiably applauded flashes of individual brilliance. But today the major football games, like the Roman circuses, function mainly as a pretext for irrationality, the regression of individuals to the tribe, to being a part of a collective, where, in the anonymous warmth of the stands, spectators can give free rein to their aggressive instincts, to the symbolic (and at times real) conquest and annihilation of the opposition. The notorious Latin American *barras bravas*, the gangs of supporters attached to certain clubs who cause havoc with their homicidal brawls and the burning of stadiums with great loss of life, show how, in many cases, it is not watching sport that attracts so many fans – almost always men, though women are increasingly attending games – but rather the ritual that releases irrational instincts, allowing them to turn their backs on civility during the game and behave as part of the primitive horde.

Paradoxically this mass phenomenon is parallel to the increased use of drugs at all levels of the social pyramid. Of course, the use of drugs has a long tradition in the West but, until recently, it has been almost exclusively confined to elites and small, marginal sectors, such as bohemian, artistic and literary circles where, in the nineteenth century, these artificial flowers were cultivated by figures as respectable as Charles Baudelaire and Thomas de Quincey.

Today, the spread of the use of drugs bears no resemblance to these earlier times; drugs are not used to explore new sensations or visions for scientific or artistic purposes. They are not an expression of rebellion against the established norms by nonconformists looking to adopt alternative forms of existence. Today, the mass consumption of marijuana, cocaine, ecstasy, crack, heroin, etc., is a response to a social environment that pushes men and women towards quick and easy pleasure, that immunizes them against worries and responsibility, allowing them to turn their backs on any self-knowledge that might be gained through thought and introspection, two eminently intellectual activities that are now considered tedious in our fickle, ludic culture. This need for distraction, the driving force of the society in which we live, stems from a desire to flee from the void and anguish that we feel when we are free, and forced to make decisions such as what to do with our lives and our world, especially in challenging times. For millions of people drugs now have the role, previously played by religions and high culture,

of assuaging doubts and questions about the human condition, life, death, the beyond, the sense or senselessness
of existence. With their artificial highs or moments of
tranquillity, drugs offer a momentary feeling of being
safe, free and happy. This is a malign fiction because
drugs isolate individuals, and only appear to free them of
problems, responsibilities and anguish. Because, in the
end, they are a form of imprisonment, demanding ever
heavier doses of stupefaction and overexcitement that
only go to deepen the spiritual void of their users.

In the civilization of the spectacle, secularism seems
to have gained ground over religions. And among those
still claiming to be believers there has been an increase
in people who just pay lip service to religion, who treat
it in a social, superficial way, but whose lives are barely
touched by it. The positive effect of the secularization
of life is that there is now greater freedom than when
ecclesiastical dogma and censorship had an asphyxiating
hold. But it would be wrong to say that, because today in
the Western world there are smaller numbers of Catholics and Protestants than before, religion has increasingly
disappeared in a secular world. That is just the stuff of
statistics. In fact, at the same time as many of the faithful were abandoning traditional religions, there was a
great increase in sects, cults, and all sorts of alternative
ways of practising religion, from Eastern spiritualism
in all its schools and divisions – Buddhism, Zen Buddhism, Tantrism, yoga – to the Evangelical churches
that now proliferate and divide and subdivide in poor

neighbourhoods, and picturesque offshoots such as the Fourth Way, Rosicrucianism, the Unification Church – the Moonies – Scientology, so popular in Hollywood, and ever more exotic and superficial churches.[1]

The reason for this proliferation of churches and sects is that only very few people can do without religion entirely. For the vast majority, religion is a necessity because it is only the security that religious faith offers on such matters as transcendence and the soul that can assuage the sense of unease, fear and anxiety in the face of extinction. And it is the case that the only way that most people understand and adhere to ethics is through religion. Only small minorities have freed themselves from religion, filling the void left in their lives by culture: philosophy, science, literature and the arts. But the culture that can fulfil this role is high culture, which confronts problems rather than shying away from them, which tries to offer serious and not playful answers to the great enigmas, questions and conflicts of human existence. Superficial and glitzy culture, which is playful and an affectation, cannot replace the certainties, myths, mysteries and rituals of religions that have stood the test

1 Let me quote from a letter from a Colombian friend: 'I have also been struck by a certain form of neo-indigenism that the upper and middle classes in Bogotá, and perhaps in other countries, are embracing as a new fashion. Now, instead of going to a priest or an analyst, these young people have a shaman and, every two weeks or so, they drink *yagé* in collective ceremonies that have a therapeutic and spiritual orientation. The participants are, of course, "atheists": cultured people, artists, old-style bohemians . . .'

of centuries. In today's society narcotics and alcohol offer a momentary spiritual peace, and provide the certainties and respite that, in earlier times, men and women could find in prayer, confession, communion and sermons.

It is also not by chance that, whereas in the past politicians on the campaign trail wanted to be photographed and appear side by side with eminent scientists and playwrights, today they look for support and endorsement from rock singers, movie actors, and football and other sports stars. Such figures have replaced intellectuals as arbiters of the political consciousness of middle and popular sectors. They present manifestos and read them at the hustings, and they appear on television preaching what is good and evil in economic, political and social spheres. In the civilization of the spectacle, the comedian is king. Furthermore, the presence of actors and singers is not just important on the periphery of political life, in the area of public opinion. Some of them have stood for election and, like Ronald Reagan and Arnold Schwarzenegger, have reached high office such as the presidency of the United States and the governorship of California. Of course, I am not discounting the possibility that film actors, rock and rap singers and footballers might make excellent contributions to the world of ideas, but I do reject the idea that their prominence in politics today has anything to do with their intelligence or their perspicacity. It is due entirely to their media presence and their acting abilities.

A notable feature of contemporary society is the

waning in importance of intellectuals who, for centuries, up until very recently, had played a significant role in the life of nations. It is often argued that the term 'intellectual' came to prominence in the nineteenth century, with the Dreyfus Affair in France and the polemics caused by Emile Zola's famous 'J'accuse', written in defence of the Jewish officer falsely accused of treason by a group of high-ranking anti-Semitic French army officers. But though the term 'intellectual' might have gained more widespread circulation from that time, the participation of thinkers and writers in public life, in debates about politics, religion and ideas, goes back to the very dawn of the West. They played a part in Plato's Greece and Cicero's Rome, in the Renaissance of Montaigne and Machiavelli, in the Enlightenment period of Voltaire and Diderot, in the Romantic era of Lamartine and Victor Hugo, and in all the historical periods leading up to modernity. Alongside their academic or creative research, many important writers and thinkers influenced political and social events through their writings, declarations and the stance they took on different issues. When I was young, this was the case with Bertrand Russell in England, Sartre and Camus in France, Moravia and Vittorini in Italy, Günter Grass and Hans Magnus Enzensberger in Germany. Such participation could be found in most countries in democratic Europe. In Spain, there are the examples of José Ortega y Gasset and Miguel de Unamuno, who played significant roles in public affairs. Today, intellectuals have disappeared from public debates, at least the debates that matter. It is true that some still sign manifestos, send letters to newspapers and become involved in polemics, but none of this has any serious repercussion in the running of society where economic, institutional and even cultural matters are decided by the political and administrative classes, and by the so-called powers that be, where intellectuals are conspicuous by their absence. Aware that they are snubbed by the society they live in, most have opted for discretion in, or absence from, public debate. Confined to their discipline or their particular concerns, they turn their back on what fifty years ago was called the civic or moral 'commitment' of writers and thinkers to society. There are exceptions but, among these exceptions, those that count – because they have media exposure – tend to be more interested in self-promotion and exhibitionism than in the defence of principles and values. Because in the civilization of the spectacle, intellectuals are of interest only if they play the fashion game and become clowns.

Why have intellectuals become so diminished and unpredictable in this day and age? One answer worth considering is the discredit that several generations of intellectuals fell into due to their sympathies with Nazi, Soviet or Maoist totalitarianism and their silence and blindness towards horrors such as the Holocaust, the Soviet Gulag and the slaughter of the Chinese Cultural Revolution. Indeed it is disconcerting and overwhelming to consider that those people who appeared to be the finest minds of their time made common cause with regimes responsible for genocide, horrendous assaults against human rights, and the abolition of every form of freedom. But the truth is that the real reason for the total loss of interest in intellectuals by society as a whole is a direct consequence of the negligible influence of ideas in the civilization of the spectacle.

A further characteristic of this civilization is the impoverishment of ideas as a driving force of cultural life. Today images have primacy over ideas. For that reason, cinema, television and now the Internet have left books to one side, and, if the pessimistic predictions of the likes of George Steiner are correct, then books will soon be relegated to the catacombs. (For the lovers of anachronistic book culture, like me, this should not be cause for lament for, if it occurs, then this marginalization might perhaps have a cleansing effect and might remove from circulation bestseller literature, justifiably called trashy literature due not only to its superficial storylines and puerile use of form, but also to its ephemeral nature, the fact that it is intended to be consumed today and then disappear, like soap or fizzy drinks.)

Cinema, of course, was always an entertainment art, geared to a mass audience. But equally, sometimes on the margins, and sometimes in the mainstream, great talents would emerge, which, despite the difficult conditions in which directors always had to work because of budget constraints and dependence on producers, were capable of making films of great richness, depth and originality, with a distinctive personal style. Today's society, by contrast, yielding to the inflexible pressure of the dominant culture, which privileges wit over intelligence, images over ideas, humour over gravity, banality over depth and frivolity over seriousness, no longer produces creators such as Ingmar Bergman, Luchino Visconti or Luis Buñuel. Who is today's cinema icon? Woody Allen, who is to David Lean or Orson Welles what Andy Warhol is to Gaugin or Van Gogh in painting or Dario Fo is to Chekhov or Ibsen in theatre.

It is also not surprising that in the era of the spectacle, special effects in film now play the leading part, relegating themes, directors, scripts and even actors to secondary roles. One might say that this is due, to a great degree, to the prodigious technological evolution of recent years, which allows for the creation of miraculous work in the field of visual simulation and fantasy. This is partly true. But it is also the case that this stems from a culture that favours minimal intellectual effort, at the expense of commitment, concern and, in the final instance, even of thought itself. This culture has given itself over, in a passive manner, to what a critic now relegated to obscurity, Marshall McLuhan – who was a wise prophet of the cultural signs of our times – called the 'image bath', a form of docile submission to emotions and sensations triggered by an unusual and at times very brilliant bombardment of images that capture our attention, though they dull our sensibilities and intelligence due to their primary and transitory nature.

Art preceded all other expressions of cultural life in

laying the foundations for the culture of the spectacle, by establishing that art could be fun and games and nothing else. Ever since Marcel Duchamp, who was clearly a genius, revolutionized the artistic values of the West by demonstrating that a urinal was also a work of art if that is what the artist decided, then everything was possible in the realm of painting and sculpture, even for a tycoon to spend over £10 million for a shark preserved in formaldehyde in a glass container, and for the author of this joke, Damien Hirst, to be revered not as an extraordinary purveyor of con tricks, which he is, but rather as a great artist of our time. Perhaps he is, but that is not to speak well of him but rather to speak very badly about our time – a time in which insolence and boastfulness and empty provocative gestures are sometimes enough, with the collusion of the mafias that control the art market and with complicit or half witted critics who confer false prestige, giving the status of artist to illusionists who hide their poverty and emptiness behind counterfeit insolence. I say 'counterfeit' because Duchamp's urinal at least had the virtue of being provocative. In our times, artists are not expected to show talent or skill but rather affectation and scandal, and their daring statements are nothing more than the masks of a new conformity. What was once revolutionary has become fashionable, a pastime, a game, a subtle acid that erodes art, turning it into a Grand Guignol show. In art this frivolity has reached alarming extremes. The disappearance of any minimal consensus about aesthetic value means that in this field confusion reigns and will continue to reign for a long time, since it is now not possible to discern with any degree of objectivity what it is to have talent or to lack talent, what is beautiful and what is ugly, what work represents something new and durable and what is just a will-o'-the-wisp. This confusion has turned the art world into a carnival where genuine creators, sharp operators and conmen all intermingle and it is often difficult to tell them apart. This is an unsettling preview of the depths to which a culture in the grip of cheap hedonism might sink as it sacrifices everything to amusement. In a perceptive essay on the frighteningly extreme tendencies in some contemporary art, Carlos Granés Maya writes that 'one of the most abject performances in Colombian memory' was performed by the artist Fernando Pertuz, who defecated publicly in an art gallery and then, 'with total solemnity', proceeded to ingest his faeces.[2]

In the area of music, the equivalent to Marcel Duchamp's urinal is, without doubt, the composition of the great guru of modernity in US music, John Cage, entitled *4'33"* (1952), in which a pianist sits in front of a piano but does not touch a note for four minutes and thirty-three seconds, since the work is comprised of the random noises produced in the hall by amused or exasperated listeners. The intention of the composer and theoretician was to abolish prejudices

---

2 Carlos Granés Maya, 'Revoluciones modernas, culpas pos-modernas', in Carmelo Lisón Tolosana, ed., *Antropología: horizontes estéticos*, Editorial Anthropos, Barcelona, 2010, p. 227.

about making value distinctions between sound and noise. There is no doubt that he succeeded.

In the civilization of the spectacle, politics has arguably become as banal as literature, film and art, which means that advertising slogans, clichés, trivia, and the latest fashion or whims now take up almost the entire space that was previously occupied by causes, programmes, ideas and doctrines. If they want to maintain their popularity, today's politicians are obliged to pay very close attention to gestures and form, which are much more important than their values, convictions and principles.

Keeping close check on wrinkles, baldness, grey hairs, the size of their nose or the whiteness of their teeth, as well as their clothes, is as important, maybe more important, to politicians than explaining their policies when elected. The arrival of the model Carla Bruni in the Elysée Palace as Madame Sarkozy, with the attendant media fireworks, shows that not even France, a country that prided itself on maintaining the old tradition of politics as an intellectual activity, a play of doctrines and ideas, has managed to hold out and has succumbed to this universally prevailing frivolity.

(As a parenthesis, I should perhaps define what I mean by frivolity. The dictionary defines frivolous as something light-hearted, capricious and insubstantial, but our age has given this form of behaviour a more complex connotation. Frivolity consists of having an inverted or unbalanced scale of values in which form is more important than content, appearance more important than essence, and in which expression and self-assurance – representation – replace feelings and ideas. In a medieval novel I admire, *Tirant lo Blanc*, the wife of Guillem de Vàroic slaps her son, a new-born baby, so that he will cry when his father sets off for Jerusalem. As readers we laugh, amused at this silliness, that the tears shed as a result of the poor creature being slapped could be confused with feelings of sadness. But neither the woman nor the characters who witness her actions laugh because for them crying – the pure form – is sadness. There is no other way of being sad than by crying – 'shedding living tears', the novel says – because in that world it is the form that counts, the content of actions are all at the service of the form. This is frivolity, a way of understanding the world, and life, where everything is appearance, theatre, play and entertainment.)

Commenting on Subcomandante Marcos's fleeting Zapatista revolution in Chiapas – which Carlos Fuentes called the first 'postmodern revolution', an acceptable definition only inasmuch as it defines the movement as mere representation, without any content or significance, staged by an expert in advertising techniques – Octavio Paz defined very precisely the ephemeral, short-term nature of the actions (or rather the simulacra) of contemporary politicians:

But the civilization of the spectacle is cruel. Spectators have no memory: for that reason they also lack remorse, or any true conscience. They embrace novelty, any novelty as long as it is new. They soon forget and move without blinking from scenes of death and destruction in the Gulf War to the curves, contortions and quiverings of Madonna and Michael Jackson. Commanders and bishops are summoned to suffer the same fate: for what awaits them also is the anonymous and universal Great Yawn, which is the Apocalypse and Judgement Day of the society of the spectacle.[3]

Our era has witnessed significant transformations in the area of sex, thanks to a progressive liberalization of old prejudices and religious taboos that kept sexual activity hemmed in by prohibitions. In this arena there has been indisputable progress in the Western world, with the freedom to choose relationships, the reduction in macho discrimination against women, gays, and other sexual minorities who have gradually become incorporated into a society that, sometimes reluctantly, is beginning to recognize the right to sexual freedom among adults. But sexual emancipation has also made the sexual act become banal: for many, above all among the younger generations, it has become a sport or a pastime, a shared activity that is no more important, perhaps less important, than going to the gym, or dancing or football. Perhaps this frivolous approach to sex is healthy in terms of psychological and emotional balance, although we should also consider that in our day and age, with its sexual freedoms, there has been no fall in sex crimes, even in the most advanced societies. If anything, they have increased. 'Light' sex

3 Octavio Paz, 'Chiapas: hechos, dichos y gestos', in *Obras Completas*, vol. V, 2nd edn, Galaxia Gutenberg/Círculo de Lectores, Barcelona, 2002, p. 546.

is sex without love and without imagination, purely instinctive and animal sex. It meets a biological need, but it does not enrich the life of the senses and emotions and it does not bring couples closer together, beyond the sexual coupling. Instead of men or women being freed from solitude, once the peremptory and fleeting act of physical love has passed, they return to solitude with a feeling of failure and frustration.

Eroticism has disappeared along with criticism and high culture. Why? Because eroticism, which turns the act of sex into a work of art, into a ritual that literature, art, music and refined sensibility have embellished with images of great aesthetic virtuosity, is the very opposite of this easy, expeditious, promiscuous sex that, paradoxically, is the result of the freedom won by the new generations. Eroticism exists as a counterpoint to or a defiance of the norm; it is a challenge to established customs and it thus implies secrecy and privacy. Out in the public glare, made commonplace, it becomes degraded and disappears, incapable of playing its former transforming role of turning sexual activity into something spiritual and artistic. It becomes pornography, that cheap, debased, obscene form of eroticism, which, in the past, had inspired a very rich tradition of literary and artistic works. These works took their inspiration in the fantasies of sexual desire and produced memorable artistic creations that challenged the political and moral status quo, fought for the rights to pleasure and gave dignity to an animal instinct, transforming it into a work of art.

In what ways has journalism influenced, and been influenced by, the civilization of the spectacle?

The border line that traditionally separated serious journalism from muckraking yellow journalism has become blurred, full of holes, and has in many cases disappeared, to the extent that it is now difficult to draw that distinction in different information media. Because one of the consequences of turning entertainment and fun into the supreme value of an era is that, in the field of information, it causes, imperceptibly, a profound upheaval in priorities: news becomes either important or of secondary interest not because of its economic, political, cultural and social significance but, above all, and sometimes exclusively, because it is new, surprising, unusual, scandalous and spectacular. Without any set intention, journalism today, following the dominant cultural mandate, seeks to offer information in an entertaining or amusing fashion, with the inevitable result that, through this subtle deformation of its traditional objectives, the press today has become light, pleasant, superficial and entertaining. And, in extreme cases, if there is not enough information of this sort around, then it can be manufactured.

For that reason it should not be surprising that the publications that reach a mass readership are not serious newspapers or journals dedicated to truth, rigour and objectivity in their news reporting but rather the so-called 'lifestyle magazines' that, with their circulations in millions, are the only example that gives the lie to the axiom that print journalism is shrinking and giving way to audio-visual and digital competition. This axiom is valid only for the press that, rowing against the tide, still seeks to be responsible and inform rather than amuse or entertain the reader. But what should we say of a phenomenon such as *iHola!* This magazine, which is now published not just in Spanish, but in eleven languages, is avidly read – or perhaps it would be more accurate to say flicked through – by millions of readers across the globe – even in the most cultured countries of the planet such as Canada and Great Britain – who, it is clearly demonstrated, enjoy reading news about how the rich, the famous and the winners in this vale of tears get married, get divorced, remarry, dress, undress, fight, become friends, spend their millions, listing their likes, their dislikes, their taste and lack of taste. I lived in London in 1989, when the English version of *iHola!*, *Hello!* magazine, appeared and I have seen with my own eyes the dizzying speed with which this creature of Spanish journalism conquered the land of Shakespeare. It would be no exaggeration to say that *iHola!* and other magazines of the same ilk are the most genuine journalistic products of the society of the spectacle.

By turning information into a form of entertainment, one gradually legitimates what had previously found refuge in marginal and almost clandestine publications: scandal, breaches of confidence, gossip, violation of privacy and – in the worst cases – libel, defamation and lies.

There is no more effective way of entertaining and amusing common mortals than by feeding their base passions. The best way to do this is by revealing the private lives of others, especially if they are well-known, prestigious public figures. This is a sport that today's journalism plays without any scruples, protected by the right to freedom of information. Although there are laws surrounding this and sometimes – very rarely – there are trials and sentences that penalize excesses, such revelations have become an increasingly widespread activity to the extent that privacy has disappeared in our day and age, and no corner of life of anyone in the public arena is immune from being investigated, revealed and exploited, to sate the voracious hunger for entertainment and amusement that newspapers, magazines and information programmes have to take into account if they want to survive and not disappear from the marketplace. While they are acting in this way to meet the demands of their public, the organs of the press are unwittingly contributing more than anyone else to consolidating this 'light' civilization that has given frivolity the supremacy previously accorded to ideas and artistic creation.

In one of his last articles, 'There is no compassion for Ingrid or Clara',[4] Tomás Eloy Martínez was incensed at the way that Ingrid Betancourt and Clara Rojas were hounded by the gutter press after their release from captivity in the Colombian jungle, six years after having been kidnapped by the FARC, with such stupid and cruel questions as whether they had been raped, or if they had seen other captives being raped or – this one addressed to Clara Rojas – if she had tried to drown in a river the son that she had with a guerrilla. 'This journalism', Tomás Eloy Martínez wrote, 'keeps insisting on turning the victims into parts of a spectacle which is presented as necessary information, but whose only function is to sate the perverse curiosity of the consumers of scandal.' His protest was fully justified, of course. But he was wrong in thinking that the 'perverse curiosity of the consumers of scandal' was a minority affair. This is not the case: this curiosity gnaws away at huge numbers of people to whom we refer when we speak of 'public opinion'. This desire for scandal, lurid details and frivolity is what gives our age its cultural tone and creates the urgent demand that the entire press, to different degrees and with different levels of subtlety, is obliged to meet, from the most serious to the most shamelessly scandalous publications.

Another topic that makes people's lives more amusing is catastrophe in its different forms. All sorts of catastrophic events are included, from earthquakes and tsunamis to serial crimes, in particular if they contain elements of sadism and sexual perversion. For that reason, today not even the most responsible press can avoid having its pages stained by blood, corpses and paedophiles. For this is the gruesome fuel that is needed to sate the appetite for amazement that the reading, listening and viewing public unconsciously demands of its media.

Of course all generalizations are fallacious and we cannot tar everything with the same brush. Of course there are differences and some media outlets try to resist the pressure under which they operate without abandoning the old principles of seriousness, objectivity, rigour and faithfulness to the truth, even if this might be boring and elicit from its readers and listeners that Great Yawn that Octavio Paz spoke about. I am pointing to a trend within contemporary journalism, though I'm fully aware that there are differences in professionalism, conscience and ethical behaviour among different press organizations. But the sad truth is that no newspaper, magazine or news programme today can survive – retain a loyal following – if it completely disregards the distinctive features of the dominant culture of the society and the time in which it operates. Of course the big press corporations are not mere weathervanes that decide their editorial stance, their moral behaviour and their news priorities simply on the basis of opinion polls on public taste. Their function is also to offer direction, assess, educate and clarify what is true and false, just and unjust, good and execrable in the dizzying vortex of today's world that their public is caught up in. But to perform this function, they must have an audience. And the newspaper or programme that does not commune on the altar of the spectacle today runs the risk of losing this audience and of addressing only ghosts.

It is not in the power of journalism by itself to change the civilization of the spectacle that it has helped to create. This reality is deeply rooted in our time. It is the birth certificate of the new generations, a way of being and living and perhaps of dying in this world of ours; we who are the fortunate citizens of countries in which the democracy, liberty, ideas, values, books, art and literature of the West have afforded us both the privilege of turning fleeting entertainment into the supreme aspiration of human existence as well as the right to view with cynicism and disdain everything that is boring or worrying, and remind us that life is not just entertainment but also drama, pain, mystery and frustration.

ELEPHANT DUNG

El País, Madrid, 21 September 1997
Translated by Natasha Wimmer

In England, believe it or not, art scandals are still possible. The very respectable Royal Academy of Arts, a private institution founded in 1768 that often presents, in its Mayfair gallery, retrospectives of great classic artists or of modern artists anointed by the critics, is these days at the centre of one that is delighting the press and the philistines who don't waste their time at exhibitions. But they'll turn out in force for this one, thanks to the scandal, thus permitting – every cloud has a silver lining – the poor Royal Academy to weather its chronic economic crises a little longer.

Was it with this end in mind that the Academy organized its *Sensation* show of works by young British painters and sculptors from the collection of the advertising magnate Charles Saatchi? If so, it was a great success. Though they may hold their noses, the masses will certainly come to have a look at the works of young Chris Ofili – twenty-nine years old, student of the Royal College of Art, and star of his generation, according to one critic – who mounts his works on bases of hardened elephant dung. It isn't for this peculiarity, however, that Ofili has made tabloid headlines, but for his blasphemous piece *The Holy Virgin Mary*, in which the mother of Jesus appears surrounded by pornographic photographs.

But it isn't this painting that has provoked most comment. That prize goes to the portrait of a famous child murderer, Myra Hindley, composed of children's handprints by the shrewd artist, Marcus Harvey. Another of the show's innovative works is a collaboration by Jake and Dinos Chapman; it is called *Zygotic Acceleration*, and – as its title implies? – it unfurls a fan of androgynous children whose faces are really erect phalluses. It goes without saying that accusations of paedophilia have been raised against the inspired authors. If the exhibition is truly representative of what inspires and concerns young artists in Great Britain, one has to conclude that genital obsession is at the top of the list. For example, Mat Collishaw has produced a work showing, gigantic in the foreground, the impact of a bullet on the human brain; but what the spectator really sees is a vagina and a vulva. And what to say about the daring creator who has crammed his glass boxes with human bones and, apparently, the remains of a foetus?

What is notable about the affair isn't that products of

this sort slip into top galleries but that people are still surprised by it. As far as I'm concerned, I noticed that something was rotten in the art world exactly thirty-seven years ago, in Paris, when a good friend, a Cuban sculptor fed up with the galleries' refusal to show the splendid wood carvings that I watched him labour over from morning to night in his *chambre de bonne*, decided that the surest route to success in art was to do something attention-catching. Immediately he produced some 'sculptures' that consisted of pieces of rotten meat in glass boxes, with live flies flying around inside. A few speakers made the buzz of the flies echo throughout the place, like a terrific threat. Sure enough, he triumphed; even Jean-Marie Drot, star of French television and radio, devoted a programme to him.

The most unexpected and disturbing consequence of the evolution of modern art and the myriad experiments feeding it is that there are no longer any objective criteria that make it possible to qualify or disqualify something as a work of art or situate it within a hierarchy. The possibility began to disappear with the cubist revolution and disappeared entirely with abstract art. Today, 'anything' can be art and 'nothing' is, depending on the sovereign whim of the spectator, who has been elevated, since the demise of all aesthetic guidelines, to the level of arbiter and judge, a position once held solely by certain critics. The only more or less generalized gauge for works of art today has nothing to do with art; it is imposed by a market controlled and manipulated by gallery cartels and dealers. Rather than reflecting tastes and aesthetic sensibilities, it revolves around publicity and public-relations campaigns and, in many cases, simple scams.

About a month ago, I attended the Venice Biennale for the fourth time in my life. (It will be the last.) I was there for a few hours, I think, and as I left I realized I would not welcome into my house a single one of all the paintings, sculptures and objects I had seen in the twenty or so pavilions I had visited. The spectacle was as boring, farcical and bleak as the show at the Royal Academy but one hundred times bigger, with dozens of countries represented in the pathetic display. Under the guise of modernity, the experiment – the search for 'new means of expression' – in reality documented the terrible dearth of ideas, artistic culture, dexterous craftsmanship and authenticity and integrity that marks a good portion of the artistic work of our times. There are exceptions, of course. But it is extremely difficult to locate them, because, contrary to the way things happen in the field of literature – where the aesthetic codes that permit the identification of originality, novelty, talent and mastery, or crudity and fraud, have not yet collapsed completely and where publishing houses still exist (for how much longer?) that maintain coherent and exacting standards – in the case of painting the system is rotten to the core. Often the most talented artists have no way of reaching an audience, whether because they refuse to be corrupted or because they are simply no good at doing battle in the dishonest jungle where artistic successes and failures are decided.

A few blocks from the Royal Academy, at Trafalgar Square, in the modern wing of the National Gallery, there is a small exhibition that should be obligatory viewing for every young person today who aspires to paint, sculpt, compose, write or make films. It is called *Seurat and the Bathers*, and it is devoted to the painting *Bathers at Asnières*, one of the artist's two most famous pieces (the other is *Sunday Afternoon on the Island of La Grande Jatte*), painted between 1883 and 1884. Although he worked on this extraordinary canvas for two years, over the course of which (as one realizes at the show) he made innumerable sketches and studies of the details and entirety of the painting, the exhibition reveals that the whole of Seurat's life was a slow, stubborn, tireless and fanatic preparation to reach the formal perfection he achieved in his two masterworks.

In *Bathers at Asnières*, that perfection astonishes and, in a way, overwhelms us: the repose of the figures sunning themselves, bathing in the river, or contemplating the scenery, beneath a midday sun that seems to dissolve the distant bridge, the locomotive crossing it, and the chimneys of Passy into the dazzle of a mirage. This tranquillity, this balance and this secret harmony between man and water, cloud and sailboat, costume and oars, are certainly manifestations of a total command of the medium, the sureness of line, and the use of colour, all achieved by dint of effort; but they also represent an elevated and noble

conception of the art of painting as a means of spiritual fulfilment and a source of pleasure in and of itself, in which
painting is understood as its own best reward, a métier in
the practice of which one finds meaning and joy. When
he finished this painting, Seurat was barely twenty-four,
the average age, in other words, of those strident young
Sensation artists at the Royal Academy; he lived only six
more years. His tiny oeuvre is one of the artistic beacons
of the nineteenth century. The admiration it arouses in
us derives from more than technical skill and meticulous
craftsmanship. Beyond all that, and somehow supporting and fostering it, is an attitude, an ethic, a manner of
surrendering oneself to the service of an ideal, which a
creator must embrace in order to transcend and extend
the limits of a tradition, as Seurat did. This way of 'choos-
ing to be an artist' seems lost for ever to today's impatient
and cynical youth, who dream of seizing glory any way
they can, even if to reach it they must climb a mountain
of pachydermatous shit.

II

A Brief Discourse on Culture

Throughout history the notion of culture has had different meanings and nuances. For many centuries it was a concept that was inseparable from religion and theological knowledge; in Greece it was characterized by philosophy and in Rome by law, while during the Renaissance it was imbued with literature and the arts. In more recent times, such as during the Enlightenment, it was science and great scientific discoveries that gave the idea of culture its particular slant. But despite these variations, and right up to the present day, culture has always signified a combination of factors and disciplines that, according to a broad social consensus, are what defines it: a recognition of a shared heritage of ideas, values, works of art, a store of historical, religious and philosophical knowledge in constant evolution, and the exploration of new artistic and literary forms and of research in all areas of knowledge.

Culture historically always established social levels between the people who cultivated it and enriched it through their different contributions, and those who showed no interest in it, scorned it or were ignorant of it, or were excluded from it for social and economic reasons. In every historical period, up to our own, there were cultured and uncultured people and, between these two extremes, there were people who were more or less cultured and more or less uncultured, and this classification was quite clear the world over because there was a shared system of values and cultural criteria, and shared ways of thinking, judging and behaving.

In our day and age all this has changed. The idea of culture has broadened to such an extent that, although nobody would dare to state this explicitly, it has disappeared. It has become an ungraspable, multitudinous and figurative ghost. Because nobody is cultured if everyone thinks they are, or if the content of what we call culture has been corrupted to such an extent that everyone can justifiably think that they are indeed cultured.

The earliest sign of this progressive muddying and confusion of what culture represents was found among anthropologists, inspired, with the best will in the world, by their desire to respect and understand the primitive societies they were studying. They established that culture was the sum total of the beliefs, knowledge, languages, customs, dress, practices, kinship networks and, in short, everything that a community says, does, fears or worships. This definition was not just limited to establishing a method for exploring the specificity of one human group in relation to another. It also desired, from the outset, to renounce the prejudiced and racist ethnography about which the West has never tired of berating itself. The intention could not have been loftier, but the well-known saying tells us that the road to hell is paved with good intentions. Because it is one thing to believe that all cultures deserve consideration because they all contribute positively to human civilization, and quite another to believe that all cultures, by the mere fact of their existence, are equivalent to each other. And this latter belief is, amazingly, what holds sway because of a huge prejudice based on the desire to abolish, once and for all, all prejudices with regard to culture. Political correctness has ended up convincing us that it is arrogant, dogmatic, colonialist and even racist to speak of superior and inferior cultures and even about modern and primitive cultures. According to this archangelic conception, all cultures, in their own way and in their own context, are equal, equivalent expressions of the marvellous diversity of humanity.

If ethnographers and anthropologists established this horizontal equivalence across cultures, erasing the classical definition of the term, sociologists – or perhaps more precisely sociologists who insist on being literary critics – for their part have carried out a similar semantic revolution, incorporating into the idea of culture, as a central component, the idea of lack of culture, disguised under the name of popular culture, a form of culture less refined, artificial and pretentious than the established form, but also freer, more genuine, more critical, representative and daring. I should say immediately that out of this process of burying the traditional idea of culture there have emerged very persuasive books such as Mikhail Bakhtin's *Rabelais and His World*. In it, with subtle logic and a range of juicy examples, the Russian critic argues that what he calls 'popular culture' serves as a sort of counterpoint to official and aristocratic culture. This culture is preserved and developed in salons, palaces, convents and libraries, while popular culture is born and lives on the street, in taverns, festivals and carnivals. Popular culture satirizes official culture, with incidents that, for example, expose and exaggerate what is hidden and censored as 'the lower stratum of the body', sex, excremental functions and coarseness, and contrasts this bawdy 'bad taste' to the so-called 'good taste' of the dominant classes.

One should not confuse the classification made by Bakhtin and other literary critics that draw on sociology – official culture and popular culture – with the division that has been current in the Anglo-Saxon world between high-brow and lowbrow culture. This latter distinction is still within the accepted classical meaning of culture, and what distinguishes the one from the other is how challenging the particular aspect of culture is to its readers, listeners, viewers or the creators themselves. A poet such as T. S. Eliot and a novelist such as James Joyce would, in this division, belong to highbrow culture while the short stories and novels of Ernest Hemingway or the poems of Walt Whitman might be considered part of lowbrow culture since they are accessible to the ordinary reader. In both these instances we are within the realms of literature itself. Bakhtin and his followers (consciously or unconsciously) did something more radical: they removed the borders between culture and lack of culture and gave lack of culture due dignity, showing that what might be seen as crude, vulgar or slovenly could be redeemed by its vitality and humour and the uninhibited and the authentic way it represented the most basic of human experiences.

In this way the borders that separated culture from lack of culture, cultured people from uncultured people, have disappeared from our vocabulary, frightened off by the thought of appearing politically incorrect. Now nobody is uncultured or, rather, we are all cultured. Just open a newspaper or magazine and see how columnists make innumerable references to the myriad manifestations of this universal culture that we all possess, with indiscriminate use of terms such as 'paedophile culture', 'marijuana culture', 'punk culture', 'Nazi aesthetic culture' and other such things. Now we are all cultured in some way, even if we have never read a book, visited an art exhibition, listened to a concert or acquired any basic idea of the humanistic, scientific or technological knowledge in the world in which we live.

We wanted to put an end to elites, which we found morally repugnant because the very word itself seemed to speak of privilege, contempt and discrimination, at odds with our egalitarian ideals. And, over time, from different positions, we were challenging and dismantling this exclusive body of pedants who thought themselves superior and boasted of having a monopoly over knowledge, moral values, spiritual elegance and good taste. But we have achieved a pyrrhic victory, a cure worse than the disease: we now live in a world of confusion, in which, paradoxically, since there is now no way of knowing what culture is, then everything is culture and nothing is.

However, you might object, never in history has there been such a host of scientific discoveries and technological advances, never have so many books been published, or so many museums opened, or such staggering prices been paid for old and modern works of art. How can we talk of a world without culture in an age in which spacecraft built by men and women have reached the stars and literacy levels are higher than at any point in history? All this progress is undeniable, but it is not the work of men and women, but rather of specialists. And between culture and specialization there is a distance as great as that between Cro-Magnon man and Marcel Proust's neurasthenic epicures. Also, although literacy levels are much higher than in the past, this is a quantitative issue, and culture has little to do with quantity, everything to do with quality. We are talking about different things. It is doubtless due to the extraordinary degree of specialization in science that we have managed to collect across the world an arsenal of weapons of mass destruction capable of destroying our planet several times over and contaminating space. This is at once a scientific and technological feat and a blatant manifestation of barbarism, that is, an eminently anti-cultural fact, if, as T. S. Eliot believed, 'culture may even be described simply as that which makes life worth living'.[1]

Culture is – or was, when it existed – a common

1 T. S. Eliot, *Notes Towards the Definition of Culture*, p. 27.

denominator, something that kept alive communication between very diverse people who had been forced, through the way knowledge has progressed, to become more specialized, that is, to become more distanced and out of touch. It was also a compass, a guide that allowed people to find their bearings in the dense thickets of knowledge without getting lost, and to have more or less clear, as this knowledge constantly developed, what were the main priorities, what was important and what not, what was the main path and what the dead ends. Nobody can know everything about everything – this was never the case, in the past or now – but for cultured people, culture at least allowed them to establish hierarchies and preferences in the fields of knowledge and aesthetic values. In an era of specialization and the collapse of culture, hierarchies have sunk into an amorphous mishmash in which – according to the latest imbroglio that classifies the innumerable forms of life baptized as cultures as equal – all forms of science and technology are justified and are deemed all the same, and there is no way of discerning with any minimum objectivity what is beautiful in art and what is not beautiful. Even to talk like this is already obsolete, because the very idea of beauty is as discredited as the classic idea of culture.

Specialists see and go further in their particular field, but they do not know what is going on around them and they do not look to identify the havoc that their achievements might cause in other areas of existence outside their own. These one-dimensional people might be at once great specialists and uncultured because, instead of connecting with others, their knowledge isolates them in a specialization that is scarcely a tiny atom in the vast field of knowledge. Specialization, which existed from the dawn of civilization, increased with the advance of knowledge, and the people who maintained social communication, those common denominators that are the glue of social interaction, were the elites, the cultured minorities who, as well as building bridges across the different areas of knowledge – science, literature, the arts and technology – also had a moral influence, be it religious or secular. For that reason intellectual and artistic progress did not become too divorced from human concerns, which looked to guarantee better opportunities and material conditions of life and a moral enrichment of society, with a decrease in violence, injustice, exploitation, hunger, illness and ignorance.

In his *Notes Towards the Definition of Culture,* T. S. Eliot argued that we should not identify culture with knowledge – he seemed to be speaking more to our age than his own, because then the problem was not as grave as it is now – because culture precedes and sustains knowledge, directs it and gives it a precise function, something akin to a moral design. As a believer, Eliot found in the values of Christian religion the support for knowledge and human behaviour that he called culture. But I do not believe that religious faith is the only possible support to prevent knowledge becoming erratic and self-destructive, like the knowledge that multiplies atomic powder kegs or contaminates with poisons the air, the earth, and the waters that sustain our lives. Since the eighteenth and nineteenth centuries, secular morality and philosophy have fulfilled this function for a broad sector of the Western world. Although it is also true that for an equal number, or perhaps a greater number, of people a belief in transcendence is a vital need in order to ward off anomie or desperation.

Hierarchies in the broad spectrum of human knowledge; morality linked to freedom, which allowed for a great diversity of expression but also firmly rejected anything that might debase and degrade basic notions of humanity and threaten the survival of the species; an elite formed not by reasons of birth or economic or political power but through work, talent and personal achievement, with the moral authority to establish in a flexible and innovative fashion priorities and values in the arts and in science and technology: this was what culture meant in the most enlightened times and societies, and this is what it should mean again if we do not want to progress, blindly and without direction, like automata, towards our own disintegration. This is the only way that life will become more liveable again for the majority of people who are in search of the always unachievable desire for a happy world.

It would be wrong to attribute identical functions to science and to the arts. It is the very fact that we have forgotten how to distinguish between them that has added to the current confusion in the field of culture. The sciences progress, like technology, wiping out whatever is old, antiquated or obsolete; for them the past is a cemetery, a world of dead things that have been surpassed by new discoveries and inventions. Literature and the arts are revitalized but they do not progress, they do not obliterate their past, but rather build on it, they draw sustenance from the past and sustain it, so that despite being so distinct and distant, Velázquez is as alive as Picasso and Cervantes is as contemporary as Borges or Faulkner.

Ideas of specialization and progress, which are inseparable from science, are inappropriate to the arts, which does not mean, of course, that literature, painting and music do not change and evolve. But one cannot say of them, as one can say of chemistry and alchemy, that the latter replaces and supersedes the former. A literary and artistic work that achieves a certain level of excellence does not die with the passing of time; it continues living and enriching new generations and evolving with them. That is why, until recently, literature and the arts were the common denominator of culture, the space where communication between human beings was possible despite differences in language, traditions, beliefs and eras, because people who today are moved by Shakespeare, who laugh with Molière and are dazzled by Rembrandt and Mozart, maintain a dialogue with those who read them, listened to them and admired them in the past.

This common space, which never became specialized, which has always been within reach of everyone, has gone through periods of great complexity, abstraction and hermeticism, which limited the understanding of certain works to an elite. But while these experimental or avant-garde works did express hitherto unknown areas of human reality and created forms of enduring beauty, they always managed to educate their readers, spectators and listeners, becoming in this way part of a common patrimony. Culture can and must also be experimental, of course, so long as the new techniques and forms that the work of art introduces broaden the horizons of life's experiences, revealing its most hidden secrets or exposing us to unknown aesthetic values that revolutionize our sensibility and give us a more subtle and novel insight into the bottomless well that is the human condition.

Culture can be experimental and reflexive, thoughtful and dreamlike, passionate and poetic, and a constant and profound critical revision of every certainty, conviction, theory and belief. But it cannot remove itself from real life, true life, lived life, which is never a life of clichés, artifice, sophism and play, carrying no risk of falling apart. I might appear pessimistic, but my impression is that, with an irresponsibility that is as great as our irrepressible desire for games and play, we have made culture into one of those showy but fragile castles built on sand, which are knocked over by the first gust of wind.

THE HOUR OF THE CHARLATANS

El País, Madrid, 24 August 1997
Translated by Natasha Wimmer

On the afternoon of the lecture by the French philosopher,

I arrived at the Institute of Contemporary Arts half an hour early to look around its bookstore, which, though tiny, I've always considered a model of its kind. But a big surprise was in store for me, because since my last visit the little place had undergone a classificatory revolution. The old-fashioned sections of earlier days – literature, philosophy, art, film, criticism – had been replaced with postmodern ones such as 'cultural theory', 'class and gender', 'race and culture', and a shelf labelled 'The Sexual Subject', which gave me a brief moment of hope but turned out to have nothing to do with eroticism, only philological patristics and linguistic machismo.

Poetry, the novel, and theatre had been eradicated; a few screenplays were the only creative form on display. Occupying a place of honour was a book by Deleuze and Guattari titled *Nomadology* and another book, apparently extremely important, by a group of psychoanalysts, jurists, and sociologists on the deconstruction of justice. Not a single one of the titles most prominently displayed (such as *Rethinking Feminist Identification*, *The Material Queer*, *Ideology and Cultural Identity*, and *The Lesbian Idol*) appealed to me, so I left without buying anything, something that rarely happens to me in a bookstore.

I had come to hear Jean Baudrillard speak, because the French sociologist and philosopher, one of the heroes of postmodernism, bears much responsibility for what is happening these days in our cultural life (if that term still has a reason to exist alongside phenomena such as the one under way at the London ICA bookstore). And also because I wanted to see him face to face, after so many years. In the late 1950s and early 1960s both of us attended the third-cycle courses given at the Sorbonne by Lucien Goldmann and Roland Barthes, and we both lent a helping hand to Algeria's FLN through the aid networks created in France by the philosopher Francis Jeanson. At that time, everyone already knew that Baudrillard had a brilliant intellectual career ahead of him.

He was extremely intelligent and expressed himself with admirable eloquence. Back then, he seemed very serious, and it wouldn't have offended him to be described as a modern humanist. I remember hearing him, in a St Michel bistro, savagely and amusingly tear apart Foucault's thesis on the non-existence of man in *The Order of Things*, which had just appeared. He had excellent literary taste, and he was one of the first in France to note the genius of Italo Calvino, in a splendid essay on Calvino that Sartre published in *Les Temps modernes*. Later, at the end of the 1960s, he wrote two dense, stimulating, long-winded, and sophisticated books that would cement his reputation, *The System of Objects* and *The Consumer Society*. From that point on, and as his influence spread around the world, setting down particularly strong roots in Anglo-Saxon countries – proof: the packed auditorium at the ICA and the hundreds of people outside who couldn't get tickets – his talent, following what seems to be the fated course of the best French thinkers of our day, has become more and more focused on an ambitious undertaking: the demolition of what is, and its replacement with a verbose unreality.

His lecture – which he began by citing *Jurassic Park* – more than confirmed this for me. The compatriots who preceded him in this labour of attack and demolition were more cautious. According to Foucault, man doesn't exist, but at least his inexistence has presence, occupying reality with its versatile void. Barthes believed that real substance could be found only in style, the inflection that each animate life is capable of imprinting on the river of words in which the self appears and disappears like a will-o'-the-wisp. For Derrida, real life is the life of texts, a universe of self-sufficient forms that modify and refer back to one another without ever coming close to addressing inessential human experience, that remote and pallid shadow of the word.

Baudrillard's sleight of hand is even more categorical. True reality doesn't exist any more; it has been replaced by virtual reality, the product of advertising and the media. What used to be called 'information' actually does the complete opposite of informing us about what is happening around us. It supplants and nullifies the real world of deeds and objective actions: they are cloned versions of what we see on television, selected and prepared by media professionals (or conjurors), and they substitute for what was once known as historical reality the objective knowledge of what is going on in the world.

Real-world events can no longer be objective. Their truth and ontological consistency are undermined from the start by the corrosive process of their projection as the manipulated and falsified images of virtual reality; these are the only images admissible and comprehensible to a humanity tamed by the media fantasy world we are born into and in which we live and die (no more and no less than Spielberg's dinosaurs). Besides abolishing history, television 'news' also vanquishes time, since it eliminates all critical perspective on what is happening: the broadcasts occur at the same time as the events they are supposedly reporting on, and these events last no longer than the fleeting instant in which they are enunciated, then disappear, swept away by others, which in turn are annihilated by new ones. This vertiginous denaturalization of the actual world has resulted, purely and simply, in its evaporation and in its replacement by the truth of media-created fiction, the only true reality of our age: the age – says Baudrillard – of 'simulacra'.

That we live in an era of large-scale representations of reality that make it difficult to understand the real world seems to me an unassailable truth. But isn't it clear that nothing, not even media mumbo-jumbo, has muddied our understanding of what is really going on in the world more than certain intellectual theories, which, like the wise men from one of Borges's lovely fantasies, pretend to embed speculative play and the dreams of fiction in real life?

In the essay he wrote proving that the Gulf War 'did not take place' – since all that business involving Saddam Hussein, Kuwait, and the allied forces was no more than television playacting – Baudrillard stated, 'What is scandalous, in our day, is not attacks on moral values, but on the principle of reality.' I wholly agree. At the same time, this seems to me an involuntary and harsh self-criticism from someone who, for many years now, has invested his dialectic shrewdness and the persuasive power of his intelligence in proving to us that audio-visual technology and the communications revolution have abolished the human ability to tell the difference between truth and lies or history and fiction, and have made us, bipeds of flesh and blood strayed into the media labyrinth of our time, mere ghostly automatons, pieces of machinery stripped of freedom and knowledge and condemned to expire without ever having lived.

At the end of the lecture, I didn't go up to say hello or to remind him of the bygone days of our youth, when ideas and books excited us and he still believed we existed.

III

Forbidden to Forbid

Some years back, in Paris, I saw a documentary on French television that left an indelible impression on me. And its images seem strikingly appropriate today, especially to debates about the most important cultural problem of our time: education.

The documentary described the problems of a school on the outskirts of Paris, one of those neighbourhoods where poor French families rub shoulders with immi grants from sub-Saharan Africa and Latin America and with Arabs from the Maghrib. This public secondary school, with a student population of both sexes drawn from a constellation of races, languages, customs and religions, had been a site of violence: attacks on teachers, sexual assaults in the toilets and in the corridors, gang fights with knives and sticks, and, if memory serves, even gunshots. I don't know if there had been any deaths, but certainly a number of injuries, and, when the police searched the place, they had seized arms, drugs and alcohol.

The documentary was looking to be reassuring, not alarmist, showing that the worst was already over and that, with the good will of the authorities, teachers, parents and students, things were getting calmer. For example, the director pointed out with undisguised satisfaction that thanks to the recently installed metal detector, which all the students went through when they entered the school, they had confiscated knuckledusters, knives and other stabbing weapons. In this way incidents of bloodletting had reduced dramatically. They had also established a rule whereby no teachers or students went round on their own, even to the toilets: they would go around in groups of two or more. This was a deterrent against attacks and ambush. And now the school had two permanent psychologists to counsel maladjusted students or recalcitrant troublemakers, who are almost always parentless or from one-parent families, from families broken apart by unemployment, promiscuity, crime and violence against women.

What most affected me in the documentary was an interview with a woman teacher who declared, quite naturally, something like: 'Tout va bien, maintenant, mais il faut se débrouiller' ('Everything is going well now, but you have to know how to cope with things'). She explained that, in order to avoid the previous attacks and beatings, she and a group of teachers had agreed to meet at a certain time, at the exit of the nearest metro, and walk to the school together. That way the risk of being attacked by *voyous* (thugs) diminished. That teacher and her colleagues, who went to school daily as if they were entering hell, had become resigned, had learned to survive and did not seem even to imagine that the life of a teacher could avoid their daily stations of the cross.

Around that time I had just finished reading one

of those enjoyable and sophisticated essays by Michel Foucault in which the French philosopher argued, with his customary brilliance, that along with sexuality, psychiatry, religion, the law and language, in the Western world education had always been one of those 'structures of power' put in place to repress and domesticate the social order, establishing subtle but very effective forms of compliance and alienation to ensure that the dominant groups in society could perpetuate their privileges and power. Well, at least in the field of education, since 1968, the castrating control over young people's libertarian instincts has been completely undermined. But, to judge from this documentary, that could have been filmed in many other places in France, and in Europe, the collapse and loss of prestige of the very idea of the teacher and of teaching – and, in the last analysis, of any form of authority – does not seem to have led to the creative liberation of young people, but, rather, to have turned these liberated schools into, at best, chaotic institutions and, at worst, mini-dictatorships ruled over by thugs and precocious criminals.

May 1968 did not put an end to 'authority', for this had been suffering a general decline for some time, in every sphere, from politics to culture, especially in the field of education. But the revolution of the rich kids, the cream of the bourgeois privileged classes in France, who were the protagonists of that amusing carnival that had as one of the slogans of the movement, 'It is forbidden to forbid', sounded the death knell of the concept of authority. And it gave legitimacy and glamour to the idea that all authority should be subject to suspicion, is pernicious and despicable, and that the most noble libertarian idea is to stand up against it, deny it and destroy it. Power itself was not affected in the slightest by this symbolic insolence of the young rebels who, without most of them knowing it, took to the barricades the iconoclastic ideals of thinkers such as Foucault. We should remember that in the first elections held in France after May '68 the Gaullist right won a resounding victory.

But authority, in the Roman sense of *auctoritas*, which is not power but rather, as it is defined in *The Spanish Real Academia Dictionary*, 'prestige and reputation which is recognized in a person or an institution, through their legitimacy or through their quality and competence in some area', never again raised its head. From then on, in Europe and in most of the rest of the world, it is almost impossible to find political and cultural figures that have both moral and intellectual influence, the classic 'authority' that teachers embodied at a popular level, a word that then had a good ring to it because it was associated with knowledge and idealism. In no other field has the effect of all this been so catastrophic for culture as in education. Teachers, stripped of credibility and authority, often singled out, from a progressive standpoint, as representatives of repressive power that had to be resisted and even shot down in order to achieve freedom and human dignity, not only lost the confidence and respect of their pupils, without which it was impossible for them to fulfil effectively their role as educators:

to transmit values as well as knowledge. They also lost the respect of parents and revolutionary philosophers, who, like the author of *Discipline and Punish*, singled out teachers as one of those sinister instruments, like prison guards and psychiatrists in mental asylums, that the establishment makes use of to bridle the critical spirit and healthy rebellion of children and adolescents.

Many teachers, with the best of intentions, believed this demonization of themselves and helped to add to the havoc, throwing buckets of oil onto the flames, by embracing some of the most ludicrous aspects of the ideology of May '68, considering it abhorrent to fail bad students, to make them repeat a course and even to give marks and establish a grade system for students' academic work because, by differentiating in this way, they would propagate the harmful notions of hierarchies, egotism, individualism, the denial of equality, and racism. It is true that these extremes have not affected every sector of school life, but one of the perverse consequences of the triumph of the ideas – the diatribes and fantasies – of May '68 has been that, as a result of this triumph, class division has become brutally accentuated within the education system.

Postmodern civilization has politically and morally dismantled the culture of our time and this explains in great part why some of the 'monsters' that we thought we had destroyed for ever after the Second World War, such as the most extreme forms of nationalism and racism, have revived and are at large once again within the heart of the West, threatening once again its values and democratic principles.

Public education was one of the great achievements of democratic, republican and secular France. In their schools and colleges, which were of a very high standard, floods of students enjoyed an equality of opportunity that corrected, with each new generation, the asymmetries and privileges of family and class, opening up for children and young people from the most underprivileged sectors the opportunity to progress, achieve professional success and political power. The state school was a powerful instrument for social mobility.

The impoverishment and disorder suffered by state education in France and in the rest of the world has given private education, which for economic reasons is accessible only to a high-earning social minority, and which has been less disrupted by the havoc caused by the so-called libertarian revolution, a defining role in the development of current and future political, professional and cultural leaders. Never was the Spanish idiom 'you never know who you are working for' more apposite. Thinking that they were acting to build a truly free society, without repression, alienation or authoritarianism, the libertarian philosophers such as Michel Foucault and his unwitting disciples instead contributed very effectively to a great education revolution, which ended up with the poor remaining poor, the rich remaining rich and the inveterate owners of power still holding the whip hand.

It is not arbitrary to quote the paradoxical case of Michel Foucault. His critical intentions were serious and his libertarian ideals were undeniable. His rejection of Western culture – which, with all its imperfections, has been responsible for the greatest development of liberty, democracy and human rights in history – led him to believe that it was more viable to achieve moral and political emancipation by throwing stones at the police and frequenting gay bath houses in San Francisco or sadomasochist clubs in Paris than through lecture halls or the ballot box. And, in his paranoid denunciation of the stratagems that, according to him, those in power used to submit public opinion to their dictates, he denied to the end the reality of Aids – the illness that killed him – as yet another trick of the establishment and its scientific agents to terrify citizens and impose sexual repression on them. His case is paradigmatic: the most intelligent thinker of his generation always had, alongside the seriousness with which he undertook his research into different areas of knowledge – history, psychiatry, art, sociology, eroticism and, of course, philosophy – an iconoclastic and provocative side (in his first essay he had sought to demonstrate that 'man does not exist'), which on occasion was just intellectual showiness, a mere gesture lacking any seriousness. Foucault was not alone in this either; he embraced a generational mandate that would define the culture of his time: a propensity for sophism and intellectual artifice.

This is another reason for the loss of 'authority' of many

thinkers of our time. They were not serious; they played with ideas and theories like circus jugglers with their scarves and clubs, who are amusing and even dazzling, but not convincing. In the field of culture they managed to produce a curious inversion of values: theory, that is, interpretation, came to replace the work of art, to become its own *raison d'être*. Critics were more important than artists; they were the true creators. Theory justified the work of art, which existed to be interpreted by the critic; it was something like a hypostasis of theory. This deification of critics had the paradoxical effect of distancing cultural criticism from the broad public, even from a cultured but not specialist public, and it has been one of the most important factors in making the culture of our time frivolous. These theorists often expressed their theories in a jargon that was esoteric, pretentious and often devoid of originality and depth, to such a degree that Foucault himself, who was not completely blameless in this regard, called it 'terrorist obscurantism'.

But the delusions of the content of certain postmodern theories – deconstructionism in particular – were at times more serious than the obscurity of the form. The thesis shared by almost all postmodern theorists, but mainly propounded by Jacques Derrida, held that the belief that language expresses reality is false. For in truth words express themselves; they offer 'versions', masks, disguises of reality, and for that reason literature does not describe the world, it merely describes itself; it is a succession of images that document the different readings of reality that books offer, using language that is always subjective and deceptive.

Deconstructionists thus subvert our confidence in any truth, in our belief that logical, ethical, cultural or political truths exist. In the final analysis, nothing exists outside language, which constructs the world that we think we know, but which is nothing more than a fiction woven of words. From there it is only a small step to state, like Roland Barthes in his 1977 inaugural lecture on being appointed to the Chair of Semiology at the Collège de France, that language is 'quite simply fascist'.

Realism does not exist and has never existed, according to the deconstructionists, for the simple reason that reality does not exist as a form of knowledge; it is no more than a tangle of discourses that instead of expressing reality hides it or dissolves it in a weft of slippery and intangible contradictions and versions, which have only relative value and contradict each other. What, then, does exist? Discourses, the only tangible reality for human consciousness, discourses that refer to each other, mediations of life or reality that can be accessible to us only through metaphors or rhetoric, with literature as the main prototype. According to Foucault, power uses these languages to control society and to nip in the bud any attempt to undermine the privileges of the dominant elites, which this power serves and represents. This is perhaps one of the most debatable theses of postmodernism. For, in truth, the most lively and creative tradition of Western culture has never been conformist. Quite the reverse:

it has offered a ceaseless questioning of existence in its entirety. It has offered a tenacious criticism of the established order, and, from Socrates to Marx, from Plato to Freud, with thinkers and writers such as Shakespeare, Kant, Dostoevsky, Joyce, Nietzsche, it has, throughout history, created artistic worlds and systems of ideas that were radically opposed to all the established powers. If we were merely the languages that power imposes on us, political liberty would not have been born, no historical evolution would have taken place, and literary and artistic originality would not have blossomed.

Of course there have been critical reactions to the fallacies and excesses of postmodernism. For example, its tendency to protect itself and seek a certain invulnerability for its theories by using the language of science received a severe setback when two real scientists, Alan Sokal and Jean Bricmont, published in 1998 *Intellectual Impostors*, a convincing demonstration of the irresponsible, inexact and often cynically fraudulent use of the sciences in the essays of philosophers and thinkers as prestigious as Jacques Lacan, Julia Kristeva, Luce Irigaray, Bruno Latour, Jean Baudrillard, Gilles Deleuze, Félix Guattari and Paul Virilio, among others. We should also remember that many years earlier – in 1957 – in his first book, *Pourquoi des philosophes?*, Jean-François Revel had virulently denounced the ways in which the most influential thinkers of the time used abstruse and pseudo-scientific language to hide the insignificance of their theories or their own ignorance.

Another severe critic of the theories and arguments of fashionable postmodernism was Gertrude Himmelfarb, who, in a polemical collection of essays entitled *On Looking into the Abyss*[1] attacked these theories, in particular the structuralism of Michel Foucault and the deconstructionism of Jacques Derrida and Paul de Man, considering them vacuous when compared to the traditional schools of literary and historical criticism.

Her work is also a homage to Lionel Trilling, the author of *The Liberal Imagination* (1950) and many other essays on culture, which were very influential in intellectual and academic circles in post-war United States and Europe, but which today very few remember and almost nobody reads. Trilling was not a liberal in the economic sphere (here he was more of a social democrat), but he was a liberal in politics, through his persistent defence of what was for him the supreme virtue of tolerance, his defence of the law as an instrument of justice, and, above all, a liberal in the cultural sphere, with his faith in ideas as a motor of progress and his conviction that great literary works enrich life, improve men and women, and underpin civilization.

For the postmoderns these beliefs are celestially naive or crassly stupid, to such a degree that nobody even bothers to refute them. Professor Himmelfarb shows that despite the few years that separate Lionel Trilling's generation from that of Derrida or Foucault, there is an

1 Alfred A. Knopf, New York, 1994.

unbridgeable abyss between them. The one is convinced that human history is singular and unitary, that knowledge is an all-embracing undertaking, that progress is possible and that literature is an activity of the imagination, rooted in history and embracing morality; while the other has relativized notions of truth and value, turning them into fictions, laying down the axiom that all cultures are equivalent, separating literature from reality and confining it to an autonomous world of texts that refer to other texts without ever relating to lived experience.

I do not share Gertrude Himmelfarb's denigration of Foucault. For all the sophisms and exaggerations that one can accuse him of, for example his theories about the 'structures of power' implicit in all language that always enact words and ideas that favour hegemonic social groups, Foucault has contributed to allowing certain marginal and eccentric manifestations (of sexuality, social repression and madness) to be openly acknowledged in the cultural sphere. But the criticisms that Himmelfarb makes of the havoc that deconstruction has caused in the humanities seem to me irrefutable. Thanks to the deconstructionists it is almost inconceivable even to talk nowadays about the humanities, for the humanities are seen as a symptom of intellectual decay and blindness.

Every time I have tackled the obscurantist prose and the asphyxiating literary or philosophical analyses of Jacques Derrida, I have felt it a miserable waste of time. This is not because I consider that every critical essay should be useful – it is enough for it to be entertaining or stimulating – but because if literature is, as he supposes, a succession or archipelago of autonomous texts, impermeable, without any possible contact with exterior reality and thus immune from all value judgement and from any interrelation with the development of society and individual behaviour, what reason is there to deconstruct them? Why all these laborious acts of erudition and rhetorical archaeology, these arduous linguistic genealogies, bringing texts together or separating them, building up these artificial intellectual deconstructions that are like animated voids? There is a complete incongruity in a critical undertaking that starts out proclaiming the essential inability of literature to have an influence on life (or be influenced by life) and to transmit truths of any kind related to the human condition and then to spend so much time painstakingly breaking down, often with insufferably pretentious intellectual flourishes, these artefacts comprised of useless words. When medieval theologians debated the sex of angels they were not wasting their time: however trivial it might seem, this question was linked in some way for them with matters as weighty as salvation or eternal damnation. But to break down some linguistic structure, whose assembly is seen, in the best of cases, as an intense formal nothingness, a verbose and narcissistic arbitrary work that teaches nothing about anything except itself, and which lacks any moral consequence, is to turn literary criticism into a gratuitous and solipsistic undertaking.

It is not surprising, in the wake of the influence of

deconstruction in so many Western universities (especially in the United States), that departments of literature have become emptied of students and have been infiltrated by so many con artists, and that there are ever-decreasing numbers of non-specialist readers for books of literary criticism (which have to be tracked down with a magnifying glass in bookshops, where they can often be found, in sleepy corners, among judo and karate manuals or Chinese horoscopes).

For Lionel Trilling's generation, by contrast, literary criticism was concerned with central questions of human existence, because they saw literature as the ultimate witness to the ideas, myths, beliefs and dreams that make a society function and to the secret frustrations or stimuli that explain individual behaviour. Their faith in the power of literature over life was so great that, in one of his essays in *Beyond Culture*, Trilling asked whether the very teaching of literature was not already, in itself, a way of denaturing the object of study. His argument is summed up in this anecdote about his students: 'I asked them to look into the Abyss [the works of Eliot, Yeats, Joyce, Proust] and both dutifully and gladly they have looked into the Abyss and the Abyss has greeted them with the grave courtesy of all objects of serious study, saying, "Interesting am I not?"'[2] In other words, the academic world froze, rendered superficial and turned into abstract

2 Lionel Trilling, 'On the Teaching of Modern Literature' (1961), in *Beyond Culture: Essays in Literature and Learning*, New York, 1965, p. 27.

knowledge the tragic and turbulent humanity contained in these profound works of imagination, depriving them of their powerful vitality, of their capacity to change the life of the reader. Professor Himmelfarb charts, in melancholic fashion, all the water that has flowed under the bridge from the time when Lionel Trilling expressed his concerns that, when turned into an object of study, literature lost its soul and its power, up to the cheerful flippancy with which Paul de Man, some twenty years later, used literary criticism to deconstruct the Holocaust, an intellectual undertaking not very dissimilar to revisionist historians who looked to deny the extermination of 6 million Jews by the Nazis.

I have reread Lionel Trilling's essay on teaching literature several times, usually when I was myself teaching. It is true that there is something deceitful and paradoxical happening when one tries to reduce imaginative writing to a pedagogical explanation, which is invariably schematic and impersonal – and to set tests that, what is worse, one then has to grade – when those works are drawn from profound and at times heartrending experiences, from real human catastrophes, which can be properly encountered, not in a lecture hall, but only in the concentrated intimacy of reading, and whose effects can be measured in the resonance that they have in the private life of the reader.

I do not remember any of my teachers making me feel that a good book takes us to the abyss of human existence and its effervescent mysteries. But some literary critics did so. I remember one above all, from the same generation as Lionel Trilling, who had on me a similar effect that he had on Gertrude Himmelfarb, influencing me with his conviction that the worst and the best of the human story could always be found in books, and that these books helped us to live. I am referring to Edmund Wilson, whose extraordinary essay on the evolution of socialist ideas and literature, from when Michelet discovered Vico to the arrival of Lenin in St Petersburg – *To the Finland Station* – came into my possession in my student years. In these luminous pages, thinking, imagining and inventing through writing were shown to be a magnificent way to act and make one's mark on history. Every chapter made it clear that great social upheavals or small individual destinies were expressed in visceral form in the impalpable world of ideas and literary fictions.

Edmund Wilson did not share Lionel Trilling's dilemma about teaching literature since he never wanted to be a university lecturer. In fact his influence spread far beyond academic circles. His articles and reviews were published in magazines and newspapers (something that a deconstructionist critic would consider an extreme form of intellectual degradation) and some of his books – including the one he wrote about the discovery of the Dead Sea Scrolls – were based on articles from *The New Yorker*. But the fact that he wrote for that profanity, a broad readership, did not mean that he lacked rigour or intellectual daring; rather, it made him try to be responsible and intelligible in his prose.

Responsibility and intelligibility go together with a certain conception of literary criticism, with the conviction that the field of literature encompasses all of human experience because it reflects it and shapes it in decisive ways, and that it should thus be the patrimony of everyone, an activity that is nurtured in the shared experiences of the species, to which we can ceaselessly refer as we search for order when we seem mired in chaos, or look for relief when we are downhearted, or explore doubts and uncertainties when reality seems too safe and reliable. By contrast, if one thinks that the function of literature is merely to contribute to the rhetorical inflation of a specialized area of knowledge, and that poems, novels and plays proliferate merely to produce certain formal disturbances in the linguistic order, then critics can wallow with impunity in the pleasures of conceptual foolery and obscurity of expression.

THE ISLAMIC VEIL

El País, Madrid, June 2003

In autumn 1987, some students attending the French school Gabriel Havez, in Creil, came to class covered by an Islamic veil and the school authorities denied them entry, reminding the Muslim girls that public education in France was secular. From that moment on there has been an intense debate in the country on this issue, a debate that has again taken centre stage with the announcement that the prime minister, Jean-Pierre Raffarin, is looking to bring to parliament a proposal that would give legal backing to the ban on wearing any religious or political garments or insignia that are 'ostentatious and proselytizing' in state schools.

When it comes to debating ideas on civic issues, France remains a model society: in the week I have just spent in France, I have followed this stimulating controversy with fascination. The matter in question has cut across established intellectual and political divisions, so that among those for and against the banning of the Islamic veil in schools, we find a mixture of left- and right-wing intellectuals and politicians in each camp, which is further proof of the increasing inanity of these rigid categories as a way of understanding ideological options in the twenty-first century. The president, Jacques Chirac, takes a different point of view from his prime minister on this issue, while opposition socialists such as ex-ministers Jack Lang and Laurent Fabius, support the prime minister. One need not be a soothsayer to understand that the Islamic veil is merely the tip of an iceberg and that what is in play, in this debate, are two different ways of understanding human rights and how democracies function.

From the outset it would appear that, from a liberal perspective – which is my position – there can be no doubt at all. The respect for individual rights demands that any person, be they a child or an adult, should be able to dress any way they like without the state getting involved in their decision, and this is a policy that applies, for example, in the United Kingdom, where, in London suburbs, some Muslim girls go to schools covered from head to toe, as in Riyadh or Amman. If all school education were privatized, the problem would not even arise: each group or community would organize its schools according to its own criteria and rules, limiting itself to following certain general state guidelines with regard to curriculum content. But this does not happen in any society, nor will it happen in the foreseeable future.

For that reason, the issue of the Islamic veil is not so simple if examined more closely and from within the framework of institutions that guarantee democracy, pluralism and freedom.

The first, irrevocable, requisite of a democratic society is the secular nature of the state, its total independence from ecclesiastical institutions, which is the only way of guaranteeing the preservation of the common interest over individual interests, and the absolute freedom of beliefs and religious practices among citizens, without any form of privilege or discrimination. One of the great conquests of modernity, in which France was at the vanguard of civilization and served as a model for other democratic societies the world over, was secularism. When, in the nineteenth century, secular public schooling was established there, it was a great step forward towards the creation of an open society, and it offered a stimulus to scientific investigation and artistic creativity, to the coexistence of ideas, philosophical systems, aesthetic currents, the development of a critical spirit and, of course, of a deep spirituality.

Because it is a grave error to suppose that a state that is neutral with respect to religious issues and secular state schooling are both looking to undermine the survival of religion in civil society. The truth is the opposite, as France itself shows, for this is a country where the percentage of believers and those practising religions – mainly Christians in the vast majority, of course – is one of the highest in the world. A secular state is not the enemy of religion; it is a state that, in order to preserve the freedom of its citizens, has removed religious practice from the public sphere into the private sphere, which is where it belongs. Because when religion and the state become confused, freedom irremediably disappears. By contrast, when they are kept separate, religion tends slowly but inevitably to become more democratic, that is, each church learns to coexist with other churches and other forms of belief, and to tolerate agnostics and atheists. This process of secularization has made democracy possible. Unlike Christianity, Islam has not experienced this process in any integral fashion, but rather in incipient, momentary ways, and this is one of the reasons why the culture of freedom has come across so many difficulties in taking root in Islamic countries, where the state is conceived not as a counterbalance to faith but rather as its servant, and often as its burning sword. And in a society where the law is sharia, freedom and individual rights vanish as they once disappeared in the *ergastula* of the Inquisition.

The girls sent by their families and communities to

French state schools wearing the Islamic veil are something more than they appear at first glance; that is, they are the advance party of a campaign undertaken by the most militant sectors of Muslim integration in France, who look to establish a beachhead not only in the education system but in all the institutions of French civil society. Their objective is to gain recognition for their right to be different, in other words, to enjoy, in public spaces, a civic extraterritoriality compatible with what these sectors consider their cultural identity, supported by their beliefs and religious practices. This cultural and political process, which hides behind the friendly exhortations to community spirit and multiculturalism made by its mentors, is one of the most potent challenges that the culture of freedom faces in our time and, in my opinion, this is the battle that has begun to be joined in France, behind the seemingly superficial and anecdotal skirmishes and run-ins between those in favour and those opposed to allowing Islamic girls to wear the veil in state schools.

There are at least 3 million Muslims living in French territory (some say many more if one takes into account illegal immigrants). And among them, of course, there are modern groups with clear democratic affiliations such as those represented by the *recteur* of the Paris Mosque, Dalil Boubakeur, whom I met a few months ago at a seminar organized by the Gulbenkian Foundation, and who impressed me with his wide-ranging cultural interests and tolerant attitude. But, unfortunately, this modern and open tendency has been defeated in recent elections to the Council for Muslim Culture and Regional Councils by radical sectors close to militant fundamentalism, who make up the Union of Islamic Organizations in France (the UOIF), one of the institutions that has campaigned most vigorously for the right of Muslim girls to attend classes in their veils, out of 'respect for their identity and culture'. This argument, taken to extremes, is endless. Or rather, if it is accepted, it will create powerful precedents for the acceptance of other practices that are so fictitiously 'essential' in their own culture, such as arranged marriages, polygamy and, as an extreme, even female circumcision. This obscurantism is dressed up in progressive garb: what right does old-style French colonial ethnocentrism have to impose, on very recent Muslim French citizens, customs and practices that are alien to their tradition, their moral codes and their religion? Clothed as self-confident pluralism, the Middle Ages might well be revived and set up an anachronistic, inhuman and fanatical enclave in the society that was the first in the world to proclaim the Rights of Man. This aberrant and demagogic reasoning must be denounced most vigorously for what it is: a very grave danger for the future of liberty.

Immigration, in our day and age, provokes exaggerated alarm in many European countries, including France, and this fear explains in great part the very high number of votes that the Front National, a xenophobic, neo-fascist movement, led by Le Pen, achieved in the last presidential election. These fears are absurd and unjustified, for immigration is absolutely essential for the economies of European countries with stagnating or declining demographics to continue growing, and for population levels to be maintained or to increase. For that reason immigration should not be seen as an incubus inhabiting the nightmares of so many Europeans, but rather as an injection of labour and creativity, to which Western countries should open their doors as widely as possible, and work for the integration of immigrants. But, of course, all this should happen without allowing that most admirable achievement of European countries, their democratic culture, to be eroded in any way, but rather to have it renewed and enriched by the adoption of these new citizens. It is obvious that it is the new arrivals that have to adapt to the institutions of freedom and not these institutions that must sacrifice themselves in order to accommodate practices and traditions that are incompatible with them. In this there should not and cannot be any concessions made in the name of the fallacies of ill-thought-out communitarianism or multiculturalism. All cultures, beliefs and customs should have their place in an open society so long as they do not collide head on with those human rights and principles of tolerance that are at the heart of democracy. The human rights and public and private freedoms guaranteed by democratic society offer a wide variety of ways to live one's life that allow for the coexistence of all religions and beliefs, but these, in many cases, must give up, as Christianity has done, the most fundamentalist aspects of their doctrine – having a monopoly, excluding others, and behaving in ways that discriminate against and damage human rights – in order to gain a democratic place in an open society. Alain Finkielkraut, Elizabeth Badinter, Régis Debray, Jean-François Revel and those who support them in this polemic are right: the Islamic veil should be banned in state schools in France in the name of freedom.

IV

The Disappearance of Eroticism

What has happened in arts and letters, and in intellectual life in general, has also happened with sex. The civilization of the spectacle has not just administered the *coup de grâce* to the old culture; it is also destroying one of its most sublime manifestations and achievements: eroticism.

One example, among thousands.

At the end of 2009 there was a small media storm in Spain when it came to light that the Junta de Extremadura, in socialist hands, had organized, within its curriculum of sex education for students, masturbation workshops for girls and boys over fourteen years of age, a programme that it entitled, somewhat mischievously, *Pleasure is in Your Hands*.

Faced with protests that this was not a good way to spend taxpayers' money, the Junta's spokespersons argued that sex education for children was necessary to 'prevent undesirable pregnancies' and that masturbation classes would 'avoid greater ills'. In the ensuing debate, the Junta de Extremadura received congratulations and support from the Junta de Andalucía: its Equal Opportunities and Social Welfare Councillor, Micaela Navarro, announced that Andalucía would soon be rolling out a similar programme. Furthermore, an attempt to close down the masturbation workshops through a legal challenge submitted by an organization close to the Popular Party, called, equally mischievously, Clean Hands, failed calamitously because the Extremadura Public Prosecutor's Office did not take up the complaint and filed it away.

Boys and girls of the world, get masturbating then! How many things have changed since my childhood when the Salesian Fathers and the La Salle Brothers – who ran the schools I went to – scared us with the idea that 'improper touching' produced blindness, tuberculosis and madness. Six decades later we have jerking-off classes in schools. Now that is progress.

Or is it really?

My curiosity sparks any number of questions. Do they take notes? Do they have examinations? Are the workshops theoretical or also practical? What feats will students need achieve to get a good grade, and what fiascos would warrant a fail mark? Would it depend on the amount of knowledge that the students could memorize, or on the speed, quantity and consistency of the orgasms produced by the girls' and boys' tactile dexterity? I am not joking. If one has the courage to set up workshops to enlighten child development in the techniques of masturbation, then these questions are pertinent.

I do not have the slightest moral reservation about the Junta de Extremadura's initiative *Pleasure is in Your Hands*. I acknowledge the good intentions behind it and I concede that, through campaigns of this sort, there might well be a reduction in unwanted pregnancies. My criticism is of a sensual and sexual nature. I am afraid that instead of liberating children from the superstitions, lies and prejudices that have traditionally surrounded sex, these masturbation workshops will trivialize it, even more than it has already been trivialized in today's society, turning sex into an exercise without mystery, dissociated from feeling and passion, thus depriving future generations of a source of pleasure that has until now nurtured human imagination and creativity.

The inanity and vulgarity that has been undermining culture has also damaged in some way one of democratic society's most important achievements in our day and age: sexual liberation, the disappearance of many taboos and prejudices surrounding erotic life. Because, as in art and literature, the disappearance of the idea of form in matters of sex is not progress but rather a backward movement that denatures freedom and impoverishes sex, reducing it to something purely instinctive and animalistic.

Masturbation does not have to be taught; it is discovered in private and it is one of the activities that comprise our private lives. It helps boys, and girls, to break out of their family environment, making them individual and sensitizing them by revealing to them the secret world of desires, and educating them on important issues such as what is sacred and what is forbidden, the body and pleasure. For that reason, to destroy the private rituals and put an end to discretion and shame, which has, since the beginning of civilization, always accompanied sex, is not to combat prejudice but rather to deprive sex of a dimension that developed around it when culture and the development of arts and letters began to enrich sex and turn it into a work of art. Taking sex out of the bedroom and exhibiting it in the public arena does not, paradoxically, liberate it but rather takes it back to caveman times when, like monkeys and dogs, couples had not yet learned how to make love, just to have sex. So-called sexual liberation, one of the most salient characteristics of modernity in Western societies, an example of which is this idea of giving masturbation classes in schools, might manage to do away with some stupid prejudices over onanism. But it might also be another stab at the heart of eroticism, perhaps with fatal consequences. Who would be the winners? Not the libertarians and the libertines, but rather the puritans and the churches. And love would go on being treated in an overblown and futile manner.

The idea of masturbation workshops is another link to the movement that, to give it a founding date (although, strictly speaking, it started earlier), began in Paris in May 1968 and that looks to do away with religious and ideological obstacles and restrictions that have, from time immemorial, repressed sex lives, leading to enormous suffering, above all for women and sexual minorities, as well as causing frustration, neurosis and other psychic disorders in people who had been the victims of discrimination and censorship, their activities condemned to precarious secrecy, due to the rigidity of the dominant moral code.

This movement has had healthy consequences, of course, in Western countries, although in other cultures, such as

Islam, the prohibitions and repression have increased. The cult of virginity that weighed so heavily on women has disappeared and thanks to this and to the extensive use of the pill, women today now enjoy if not exactly the same freedom as men, at least a degree of sexual autonomy infinitely greater than their grandmothers and great grandmothers and their contemporaries in Muslim and Third World countries. Furthermore, even though they have not completely disappeared, there has been a great reduction in prejudice, hostility, and in the laws that, until recently, penalized homosexuality as a perversion. Gradually Western countries are allowing same-sex marriages, with the same rights as heterosexual couples, including the right to adopt. And also, slowly, an idea is gaining ground that, in sexual matters, what adults of sound mind do or do not do is their decision and nobody else's and that nobody, from the state to the Church, should interfere in this matter.

All this is progress, of course. But it is wrong to believe, like the promoters of this liberation movement, that by demystifying sex, stripping it of the veils, the modesty and the rituals that have been part of it for centuries, abolishing any symbolic form of transgression in the sexual act, it would then become a healthy and normal activity in society.

Sex is healthy and normal only among animals. It was this way for bipeds, before we were completely human, that is when sex was little more than instinct, a physical discharge of energy that guaranteed reproduction. The move away from an animal state was a long and complex process for the species and in this process a decisive role was played by what Karl Popper called 'the third world', the world of culture and invention, the gradual emergence of sovereign individuals, their emancipation from the tribe, with leanings, aptitudes, wishes, desires that differentiated them from others and defined them as singular beings. Sex played a decisive role in the creation of the individual and, as Sigmund Freud has shown, in this domain, the most recondite area of individual sovereignty, the distinctive features of every personality are developed, that which belongs to each of us and makes us different from others. It is a private and secret domain and we should try to keep it this way if we do not wish to cut off one of the most intense sources of pleasure and creativity, that is, of civilization itself.

Georges Bataille was not wrong when he warned against the risks of excessive permissiveness in sexual matters. The disappearance of prejudices, which is doubtless liberating, cannot mean the abolition of the rituals, the mystery, the forms and the discretion through which sex became civilized and human. With sex as public, healthy and normal, life would become more boring, mediocre and violent than it is now.

There are many ways to define eroticism, but perhaps the main way would be to call it physical love stripped of animality, its conversion – through time and thanks to the development of freedom and the influence of culture in private life – from the satisfaction of an instinctive urge into a creative shared activity that prolongs and sublimates physical pleasure, providing a *mise en scène* and refinements that turn it into a work of art.

Perhaps there is no other activity that has established such an obvious dividing line between the animal and the human as sex. In the beginning, in the night of earliest times, this difference did not exist and both were conjoined in a physical coupling without mystery, without grace, without subtlety and without love. The humanization of the lives of men and women is a long process in which the advance of scientific knowledge and philosophical and religious ideas played their part, as did the development of arts and letters. Over this period nothing has changed as much as our sex lives. This has always been a stimulus of artistic and literary creation and, in reciprocal fashion, painting, literature, music, sculpture, dance, all the artistic manifestations of human imagination, have contributed to the enrichment of pleasure in sexual activity. It would not be outrageous to say that eroticism marks a high point of civilization and that it is one of civilization's defining characteristics. To gauge how primitive a community is or how far it has advanced in civilization there is no better way than by scrutinizing the secrets of the bedroom and finding out how its inhabitants make love.

Eroticism does not only have the positive and dignifying function of adding beauty to physical pleasure, opening up a wide range of suggestions and possibilities through which human beings can satisfy their desires and fantasies. It is also an activity that brings to the surface those spectres hidden in the irrational part of our natures that are lethal and destructive. Freud called this destructive urge Thanatos, which is in constant conflict within us with the vital and creative instinct, Eros. Left to themselves, without any curbs, these monsters of the unconscious that surface in sex and demand their rights could lead to dramatic violence (like the violence that bathes in blood and litters with corpses the novels of the Marquis de Sade) and even to the extinction of the species. That is why eroticism does not just consider prohibition as a voluptuous stimulus but also as a boundary, which could lead to suffering and death if transgressed.

I discovered that eroticism was inseparably bound up with human freedom but also with violence through reading the great masters of erotic literature in the collection *Les Maîtres de l'amour*, directed by Guillaume Apollinaire (who wrote prologues to and translated some of the volumes).

It happened in Lima, around 1955. I had just got married for the first time and I had to take on different jobs to earn a living. I ended up with eight jobs, while I continued my university studies. The most colourful of these was cataloguing the dead whose names had disappeared from the archives of the Beneficencia (Record Office) in the colonial area of the Presbítero Maestro cemetery in Lima. I did this on Sundays and on holidays, going to the cemetery equipped with a small ladder, index cards and pencils. After completing my examination of the old stones, I compiled lists with names and dates and the

Beneficencia Pública paid me for each dead person. But the most enjoyable of my eight jobs that earned my daily bread was not the cemetery but acting as assistant to the librarian of the Club Nacional. The librarian was my university teacher, the historian Raúl Porras Barrenechea. My duties consisted of spending two hours daily, from Monday to Friday, in the elegant building of the Club, the symbol of the Peruvian oligarchy, which, around that time, was celebrating its centenary. In theory, I was supposed to spend these two hours cataloguing the new additions to the library but, I don't know if through lack of funds or through negligence, the Club Nacional hardly acquired any new books in those years, so I could spend these two hours writing and reading. These were my two happiest hours in those days during which, from early morning until night, I never stopped doing things that interested me little or not at all. I did not work in the beautiful reading room on the ground floor of the Club; I was in an office on the fourth floor. There I discovered, with delight, hidden behind some discreet folding screens and prim little curtains, a splendid collection of erotic books, almost all French. There I read the letters and erotic fantasies of Diderot, Mirabeau, the Marquis de Sade, Restif de la Bretonne, Andréa de Nerciat, Aretino, *The Memoirs of a German Opera Singer*, *The Autobiography of an Englishman*, *The Memoirs of Casanova*, *Dangerous Liaisons* by Choderlos de Laclos and any number of other classic and emblematic works of erotic literature.

Erotic literature had classical antecedents, of course,

but it really came to the fore in eighteenth-century Europe, in the heyday of the *philosophes* and their great innovative theories on morality and politics, their offensive against religious obscurantism and their passionate defence of freedom. Philosophy, sedition, pleasure and freedom were what these thinkers and artists demanded and practised in their writings, embracing with pride the term 'libertine' that was used to describe them, bringing to mind that the main meaning of this word was, according to Bataille, 'the person who defies or disobeys God and religion in the name of liberty'.

Libertine literature is very uneven, of course; there are few great works among them, although one can find some very interesting novels or texts among the majority of those with little or no literary merit. The main limitation, which detracted from their worth, is that, when they concentrate in an obsessive and exclusive manner on the description of sexual experiences, books that are *solely* erotic soon succumb to repetition and monomania, because sexual activity, while being an intense and marvellous source of pleasure, is limited, and if it is separated out from the rest of the activities and functions that make up the lives of men and women, then it loses vitality and becomes a limited, caricatural and inauthentic depiction of the human condition.

But this does not mean that libertine literature must always be seen as a cry of freedom against all forms of subjugation and servitude – religious, moral or political – that restrict the right to free will, to social and political freedom and to pleasure, a right that was demanded for the first time in the history of civilization: to be able to materialize the fantasies and desires that sex awakens in human beings. The great merit of the monotonous novels of the Marquis de Sade is to show how sex, if practised without any limits or breaks, leads to deranged violence because it is the main channel through which the most destructive instincts of personality are manifest.

The ideal thing in this respect would be for the boundaries within which our sex lives unfold to broaden sufficiently for men and women to act freely, exploring their desires and fantasies without feeling threatened or discriminated against, but within certain cultural forms that preserve the private and intimate nature of sex, so that sex lives do not become banal or animalistic. That is eroticism. With its rituals, fantasies, its clandestine nature, its love of form and theatricality, it emerges as a product of high civilization, a phenomenon inconceivable in primitive or rudimentary societies or people, because it is an activity that requires refined sensibility, literary and artistic culture and a certain propensity for transgression. Transgression is a word that has to be taken with a pinch of salt in this case since, within the context of eroticism, it does not mean a denial of the dominant moral or religious code but rather both the recognition and the rejection of this code, blended in seamless fashion. Violating the norm in an intimate setting, with discretion and through common accord, the couple or the group perform a representation, a theatrical game that inflames their pleasure, fanned by defiance and freedom, while also maintaining the concealed, confidential and secret nature of sex itself.

Without attention to the forms, to the ritual that enriches, prolongs and sublimates pleasure, the sex act would become again a purely physical exercise – a natural drive in the human organism, where men and women are merely passive instruments – devoid of sensitivity and emotion. A good illustration of this today can be found in the trashy literature that purports to be erotic, but achieves only the vulgar rudiments of the genre: pornography. Erotic literature becomes pornographic for purely literary reasons: a sloppy use of form. That is, when writers are negligent or clumsy in their use of language, their plot construction, their use of dialogue, their description of a scene, they reveal inadvertently everything that is crude and repulsive in a sexual coupling devoid of feeling and elegance – without a *mise en scène* or ritual – turned into something that is the mere satisfaction of the reproductive instinct.

Making love in our time, in the Western world, is much closer to pornography than to eroticism and, paradoxically, it has become a degraded and perverse derivate of freedom.

The masturbation workshops that young people will attend in the future as part of their school curriculum might appear to be a daring step forward in the struggle against priggishness and prejudice in matters of sex. In reality it is likely that this and other initiatives designed to demystify sex, making it something as common and everyday as eating, sleeping and going to work, might have the effect of making future generations feel prematurely disillusioned by sex. For sex would lose its mystery, passion, fantasy and creativity and would become banal, a gymnastic workout. And this could lead to young people looking for pleasure in other areas, probably in alcohol, violence and drugs.

If we want physical love to enrich people's lives, let us free it from prejudices but not from the forms and rites that embellish it and civilize it. And instead of exhibiting it broad daylight, let us preserve that privacy and discretion that allows lovers to play at being gods and feel that they are gods in those intense and unique instances of shared passion and desire.

THE PAINTER IN THE BROTHEL

El País, Madrid, 1 April 2001

Jean-Jacques Lebel, a writer and avant-garde artist who used to organize 'happenings' in the 1960s, had the very daring idea back then to stage, 'with absolute fidelity', *Desire Caught by the Tail*, a delirious theatre piece written by Picasso in 1941 in which, among other crazy things, a female character, La Tarte, urinates on stage for ten consecutive minutes, squatting over the prompter's booth. (To achieve this effect, Lebel informs us, the liquefying actress had to drinks pints of tea and great infusions of cherries.) He talked to the painter at the beginning of 1966 about the project and Picasso showed him a whole raft of erotic drawings and paintings, from his Barcelona period, that he had never exhibited. From that moment Lebel decided that one day he would organize an exhibition that would show, without any equivocation or censorship, the power of sex in Picasso's world.

This idea has finally become a reality, almost four decades later, in a vast exhibition of 330 works, many of them never exhibited before, in the Jeu de Paume in Paris, where it will stay until the end of May, before moving on to Montreal and Barcelona. The first question to ask, after going round this exciting exhibition (never has that adjective been more appropriate), is why it has taken so long to organize. There have been innumerable exhibitions on the work of this artist, whose influence can be found in every branch of modern art, but, until now, nothing specific on the theme of sex, which, as this exhibition curated by Lebel and Gérard Régnier so very clearly demonstrates, obsessed the painter in a very productive way. Especially at certain extreme moments in his life – in his youth and old age – he experimented and expressed himself in this area with remarkable confidence and daring, in drawings, sketches, objects, engravings and canvases that, despite their uneven artistic value, reveal his most secret and intimate motivations – his desires and erotic fantasies – and throw a new light on the rest of his work.

'Art and sexuality are the same thing,' Picasso said to

Jean Leymarie and, on another occasion, he pointed out that 'there is no such thing as chaste art'. Perhaps such remarks might not be true for all artists, but they are quite clearly appropriate for him. Why, then, did Picasso himself help to hide for quite a long time this aspect of his artistic production, which is a constant in his work, even though at times he chose to keep it a secret? For ideological and commercial reasons, says Jean-Jacques Lebel in an interesting interview with Geneviève Breerette. During his Stalinist period, when he painted the portrait of Stalin and denounced the 'massacres in Korea', eroticism would have been a source of conflict between Picasso and the Communist Party, to which he was affiliated, and which espoused the aesthetic orthodoxy of socialist realism, in which there was no room for the 'decadent' celebration of sexual pleasure. And late, following the advice of his agents, he admitted that he kept this aspect of his work hidden for fear of offending the puritanism of US collectors, thus cutting off this lucrative market. These are human weaknesses that geniuses are not exempt from, as we know. In any event, it is now possible to consider every facet of Picasso's work, a universe with so many constellations that it makes us giddy. How could one hand, the imagination of a single mortal, produce such extraordinary creativity? There is no reply to this question; Picasso leaves us speechless, as do Rubens, Mozart or Balzac. The development of his work, with its distinctive stages, themes, forms and motifs, is a journey through all the schools and artistic movements of the twentieth century, which he learned from and to which he contributed in his own completely distinctive way. Then he looked to the past, bringing that past back into the present in a number of very finely observed recreations, caricatures and rereadings that showed just how contemporary and fresh the Old Masters were. But sex is never absent, in all the periods into which critics have divided and organized Picasso's work, even in the Cubist years. Sometimes it is a discreet, symbolic reference, working through allusion. At other times it is insolently open and crude, in images that seem to challenge the conventions of eroticism, refinement and the chaste ways that art has traditionally described physical love, to make it compatible with established morality.

The sex that Picasso reveals in most of these works, especially in the years of his youth in Barcelona, is elemental, not sublimated by the rituals and baroque ceremonies of a culture that disguises, civilizes and turns animal instinct into works of art, a sex that wants desire immediately satisfied, without delay, subterfuge, fuss or distractions. Sex for the hungry and the orthodox, not sex for dreamers or refined people. That is why it is a completely macho sexual outlook, where there is no male homosexuality and where lesbianism is just there for the pleasure of the male onlooker. Sex for men, primitive, rough, where the phallus is king. Women are there to serve, not to have pleasure themselves, but to give pleasure, to open their legs and submit to the whims of the fornicating male. They are often depicted kneeling, engaged in fellatio, which could be seen as an archetypal image of this sexual order: the woman gives pleasure but also yields to and adores the all-powerful macho. The phallus, these images proclaim, is above all else power.

It is natural that the privileged location for this sort of pleasure is the brothel. There are no sentimental distractions in the way of this drive that looks to sate an urgent need and then forget about it and go on to something else. In the brothel, where sex is bought and sold, where there are no entanglements and no excuses or alibis are necessary, sex is revealed in all its naked truth, as pure present, as an intense and shameless spectacle that does not linger in the memory, pure and fleeting copulation, immune to remorse and nostalgia.

The repeated images of this brothel sex, its vulgarity and lack of imagination, that fill so many notebooks, cards and canvases, would be monotonous without the cheerful touches that we find, jokes and exaggerations that show a state of mind brimming over with enthusiasm and happiness. A humanized fish – a mackerel! – is licking a young woman who is compliant but bored to death. And in all this work, even the rapid sketches he did in the middle of some party, on serviettes, menus and newspaper cuttings, to please a friend or to record a meeting, there is evidence of his extraordinary craft, that piercing gaze that can set down in a few essential brushstrokes the mad vortex of reality. The apotheosis of the brothel in Picasso's work is, of course, *Les Demoiselles d'Avignon*, which is not in this exhibition, although many of the first sketches and drafts of this masterpiece are here.

With the passing of the years, the rough sexual edges of youth were smoothed out, and desire began to be expressed in mythological characters. All the Minotaurs painted in the 1930s gleam with vigorous sensuality, with a sexual power that displays its bestiality with grace and shamelessness, as a proof of life and artistic creativity. By contrast, in the beautiful series of prints dedicated to Raphael and La Fornarina from the late 1960s, the loving interaction between the painter and his model under the lascivious gaze of an old pontiff who is resting his flaccid limbs on a chamber pot, is imbued with a deep sadness. What is represented here is not just the joyful physical love of the young people, the voluptuousness that is part of artistic endeavour. There is also the melancholy of the observer, who, with the passing of the years, is no longer competing in the jousts of love, an ex-combatant who must resign himself to enjoy looking at other people's enjoyment, while he feels life slipping away. And that the death of his sexual drive will soon be followed by the other, the definitive death. This theme is recurrent in the final years of Picasso's life, and the exhibition in the Jeu de Paume has a number of pictures in which this inconsolable nostalgia for a lost virility appears with a wrenching insistence, the bitterness of knowing that the fateful wheel of time no longer allows one to bathe in the source of life, to experience that explosion of pure pleasure in which human beings glimpse immortality and which the French ironically call 'the little death'. Figurative death and real death, orgasm and physical extinction, are the protagonists of the dramatic painting that Picasso kept on producing almost until the final death rattle.

COLD SEX

El País, Madrid, 27 May 2001

The story goes that, on his wedding night, the young Victor Hugo made love eight times to his wife, the chaste Adèle Foucher. And that as a consequence of that record set by the ardent author of *Les Misérables* who, according to his own confession, had come a virgin to the nuptial bed, Adèle was immunized forever against this type of activity. (Her tortuous adulterous adventure with the ugly Sainte-Beuve was not about pleasure but about spite and revenge.)

The philosopher Jean Rostand laughed at Hugo's record, comparing it with the feats of fornication achieved by other species. What, for example, are eight consecutive effusions of the Romantic bard compared with the forty days and nights that a toad copulates with his mate, without pausing an instant to take a break? Now, thanks to a battle-hardened French woman, Ms Catherine Millet, anura amphibians, rabbits, hippopotamuses and the other great fornicators of the animal kingdom have met, from within the mediocre human species, a rival able to take them on on equal terms, and even to defeat them in the copulation stakes.

Who is Ms Catherine Millet? A distinguished art critic for more than half a century, she is the managing editor of *Art Press* in Paris, and the author of studies on conceptual art, the painter Yves Klein, the designer Roger Tallon, contemporary art and avant-garde criticism. In 1989 she was the commissioner of the French section at the São Paulo Biennale and, in 1995, the commissioner of the French pavilion at the Venice Biennale. Her celebrity, however, is more recent. It comes from an autobiographical essay on sex, recently published by Seuil, *La vie sexuelle de Catherine M.*, which caused a considerable stir and was at the top of the bestseller list in France for several weeks.

I must say straight away that Ms Millet's essay is considerably more interesting than the ridiculous clamour surrounding it, and that those who rushed to read it, attracted by the aura of eroticism and pornography that surrounded it, were to be disappointed. The book is not a sexual stimulant, nor does it offer an intricate imagery of erotic rituals. It is rather an intelligent, crude, unusually frank memoir that takes on, at times, the appearance of a clinical report. The author looks over her own sex life with the glacial and obsessive dedication of those miniaturists who make boats within bottles or paint landscapes on the head of a pin. I will also say that the book, albeit interesting and worthy, is not pleasant to read because the view of sex that it leaves the reader with is almost as tiring and depressing as that formed by Madame Victor

Hugo after her eight marital encounters on her wedding night.

Catherine Millet began her sex life quite late – at seventeen – for a girl of her generation, growing up in the great revolution in behaviour symbolized by May '68. But she immediately started making up for lost time, making love, on all sides and through every conceivable part of her body, at a dizzying pace, until she reached totals that must have far exceeded the thousand women boasted of by the incontinent Belgian author Georges Simenon.

I insist on the quantitative factor because she does so in the extensive first part of the book, entitled, precisely, 'The Number', where she documents her predilection for *partouses*, promiscuous sex, sex in groups. In the 1970s and 1980s, before sexual liberation lost its impetus and, with the spectre of Aids, stopped being fashionable throughout Europe, Ms Millet – who describes herself as a timid, disciplined, rather docile woman – found a form of communication with her fellows through sexual relations that she found difficult in other aspects of life. She made love in private clubs, in the Bois de Boulogne, at roadsides, in the hallways of buildings, on public benches, as well as in private houses and, once, in the back of a van where, with the help of her friend Eric, who organized the queue, she dispatched dozens of solicitants in a few hours.

I say solicitants, because I don't know what to call the author's fleeting and anonymous co-adventurers. Not clients, of course, because Catherine Millet, although she has bequeathed her favours with boundless generosity, has never charged for doing so. Sex for her has always been enthusiasm, sport, routine, pleasure, never a profession or a business. Despite the unbridled way she has had sex, she says that she was never the victim of abuse and never felt in danger: even in situations that flirted with violence, it was enough for her to offer a simple negative reaction for her wishes to be respected. She has had lovers and now has a husband – a writer and photographer who has published an album of naked photos of his wife – but a lover is someone that presupposes a somewhat stable relationship, while most of Catherine Millet's sexual companions appear as passing shadows, casually taken and abandoned, almost without any words passing between them. Individuals with no name, face or history, the men who pass through this book are, like the furtive vulvas in libertine literature, no more than transient cocks. Until now, in confessional literature, only men made love like this, in blind sequence and in bulk, without even bothering to know with whom. This book shows – and perhaps this is what is really scandalous about it – that it was wrong to believe that conveyor-belt sex, turned into strict sexual gymnastics, completely devoid of feeling and emotion, was the exclusive domain of anything in trousers.

It is important to say that in these pages Catherine Millet shows no traces of being a feminist. She does not display her very rich experience in sexual matters as a flag of protest, or as an accusation against the prejudice and discrimination that women still suffer in the sexual domain. Her testimony is in no way strident and has no pretensions to illustrate, in its account, some general ethical, political or social truth. Quite the reverse, hers is an extreme individualism, very visible in her obsession with not wanting to draw from her experiences any general conclusions, doubtless because she thinks that there are none. Why then has she made public now, in this unprecedented autopsy on herself, this intimacy that the vast majority of men and women keep hidden under lock and key? It would seem that by so doing she wants to see whether she will be better understood, and able to transform into knowledge, into clear and coherent ideas, that dark well of actions, seizure, audacity, excesses and, also, confusion, which, despite the freedom with which she has embraced it, sex still means for her.

What is most disconcerting in this memoir is the coldness with which it is written. The writing style is efficient, committed to being lucid, and often abstract. But the coldness does not just permeate the mode of expression and the argument. It is also the material, the sex that exhales an air of coldness, which, in many pages, is also depressing. Ms Millet assures us that many of her associates satisfy her, help her to materialize her ghosts, and that she has a good time with them. But do they really fulfil her, give her pleasure? The truth is that her orgasms seem mechanical, resigned and sad. She herself seems unequivocally to confirm this impression in the final pages of the book when she points out that, despite the diversity of people with whom she has made love, she has never felt so sexually fulfilled as when ('with the regularity of a civil servant') she masturbated. So that widespread macho (now this adjective is open to debate) belief that only variety can bring pleasure in sex is not always true. Let Ms Millet tell you: none of her innumerable flesh-and-blood partners have been able to depose her incorporeal ghosts.

This book confirms what all literature that focuses on sex has shown over and over again: that, if separated from all the other activities and functions that make up our existence, sex is extremely monotonous, so limited in its scope that, in the end, it is dehumanizing. A life in thrall to sex, to sex alone, reduces this function to an organic primary activity, no more noble or pleasurable than drinking for the sake of drinking, or defecating. It is only when culture civilizes it and charges it with emotion and passion, and clothes it in ceremonies and rituals, that sex can enrich human life enormously and have a beneficial effect on all the twists and turns of existence. For this sublimation to occur, it is essential, as Georges Bataille has explained, that certain taboos and rules that can channel and limit sex should be preserved, so that physical love can be lived – enjoyed – as transgression. Unrestricted freedom, the abandonment of all theatre and convention in the activity of sex, has not enriched the pleasure and happiness that we humans experience through sex. It has rather contributed to making it banal, converting physical love, one of the most fertile and enigmatic sources of humanity, into a mere pastime.

Furthermore, we should not forget that this sexual activity that unfolds with such eloquence in Catherine Millet's account is still the domain of small minorities. At the same time as I was reading her book, there was an account in the press of the execution in Iran of a woman who had been found guilty by a court of ayatollahs of appearing in pornographic films. We should be clear that 'pornography' in a fundamentalist Islamic theocracy consists of a woman revealing her hair. The guilty woman, according to the law of the Koran, was buried in a public square up to her chest, and stoned to death.

V

Culture, Politics and Power

Culture does not depend on politics, or it should not, although this is inevitable in dictatorships, especially in ideological or religious dictatorships, in which the regime feels authorized to dictate norms and establish canons of behaviour within which cultural life evolves, under the vigilance of the state, which is committed to making sure that cultural life does not stray from the orthodoxy that supports the regime. The result of such control, as we know, is the progressive transformation of culture into propaganda. In these conditions culture withers, starved of originality, spontaneity, critical thinking, with no opportunity for renewal and formal experimentation.

In an open society, even if culture maintains its independence from official concerns, it is inevitable and necessary that culture and politics are connected and interact. Not just because the state, without impinging on creative and critical freedom, should support and promote cultural activities – above all by preserving and promoting cultural heritage – but also because culture should exert an influence over political life, submitting it to a continual critical evaluation and inculcating it with values to prevent it from becoming degraded. Unfortunately, in the civilization of the spectacle, the influence that culture exerts over politics does not help it to maintain certain standards of excellence and integrity but instead contributes to its moral and civic decline, stimulating its worst aspects, including, for example, bad acting. In the prevailing culture, politics has been increasingly replacing ideas and ideals, intellectual debate and programmes, with mere publicity and an obsession with physical appearance. As a consequence, popularity and success are achieved not so much through intelligence or probity as through demagogy and a talent for histrionics. We are thus left with the curious paradox that while in authoritarian societies it is politics that corrupt and degrade culture, in modern democracies it is culture – or what usurps the name – that corrupts and degrades politics and politicians.

To illustrate my point more clearly, I will step back in time and speak of public life in the context that I know best: in Peru.

When I first attended the University of San Marcos, in 1953, 'politics' was a dirty word in Peru. The dictatorship of General Manuel Apolinario Odría (1948–56) had created a situation whereby, for a great number of Peruvians, 'getting into politics' meant becoming involved in a criminal activity, associated with social violence and illegal actions. The dictatorship had imposed a Law of Internal Security in the Republic that outlawed all parties, and a rigorous censorship prevented the slightest criticism of the government appearing in newspapers, magazines or on the radio (television had not yet arrived). Instead, all the news outlets teemed with praise for the dictator and his accomplices. Good citizens were those who concentrated on their work and their domestic life without getting involved in public life, which was a monopoly of those who held power, protected by the armed forces. Repressive policies imprisoned APRA, Communist and trade union leaders. Hundreds of militants from these parties along with people linked to the democratic government of Dr José Luis Bustamante y Rivero (1945–8), which had been overthrown by Odría's military coup, were forced into exile.

There was some clandestine activity, but it was minimal, due to the severity of the repression. The University of San Marcos was one of the most intense foci of these catacomb activities, carried out almost exclusively by Apristas and Communists, who were bitter rivals. But these were a small minority among the student body, which, out of fear or apathy, also subscribed to the dominant apolitical mood that, as in all dictatorships, the Odría government looked to impose on the country.

From the mid-1950s the regime became increasingly unpopular. And, as a consequence, increasing numbers of Peruvians dared to become politically active, to stand up to the government and its thugs and the police force in meetings, strikes, stoppages, and through printed manifestos, forcing it to call elections, which, in 1956, put an end to the eight-year regime.

With the re-establishment of the rule of law, the repeal of the Law of Internal Security, the restoration of press freedoms, the reintegration of outlawed parties and the creation of new parties – the Popular Action Party, the Christian Democrats and the Progressive Social Movement – politics took centre stage again, rejuvenated and enjoying a new prestige. As often happens when a dictatorship is replaced by a democratic regime, civic life attracted many Peruvian men and women as a way to heal the country's ills. It is not an exaggeration to say that in those years the most eminent professionals, businessmen, academics and scientists felt called to become involved in public life, driven by a selfless desire to serve Peru. This can be seen in the parliament elected in 1956. From then on, Peru has never had a Senate and a Chamber of Deputies of such high intellectual and moral quality. Something similar can be said of the people who were cabinet members or held public office in those days, or who, from the opposition benches, engaged in politics, criticizing the government and offering alternatives to government policy.

I am not saying that the governments of Manuel Prado (1956–62) and of Fernando Belaúnde Terry (1963–8) – with an interlude of a military junta (1962–3) so as not to lose the habit – were successful. They clearly were not since, in 1968, this brief democratic parenthesis of little more than a decade was interrupted once again by a military dictatorship – led by General Juan Velasco Alvarado and General Francisco Morales Bermúdez – which would last for twelve years (1968–80). What I wish to stress is that, from 1956 and for a brief period, politics in Peru was not perceived by society as an insignificant matter, but instead attracted a large number of people who saw in it an activity that could channel energies and talents capable of turning this backward and impoverished society into a free and prosperous country. Politics became decent for a few years because decent people decided to become involved in politics instead of avoiding it.

Today, in all the opinion polls on politics, a significant number of citizens state that it is a mediocre and grubby activity that puts off the most honest and capable people and instead mainly recruits nonentities and rogues who see politics as a quick way of becoming rich. This is not unique to the Third World. The loss of prestige in politics knows no borders and speaks to an irrefutable reality: while acknowledging variants and nuances in individual countries, throughout almost the entire world, both developed and underdeveloped, the intellectual, professional and doubtless also moral level of the political class has declined. Dictatorships are not alone in this. Democracies suffer from the same decline, and the consequence is a lack of interest in politics that leads to the low participation in elections that we witness so frequently in most countries. There are very few exceptions. Probably there are no longer any societies in which the best people are attracted to civic duties.

Why has the entire world come to believe what all dictatorships have sought to instil in the people they oppress, that politics is an unworthy activity?

It is the case that, in many places, politics is, or has

become, sullied and debased. "Twas ever thus," say the pessimists and cynics. No, it was not always that way, nor is it now true everywhere and in the same way. In many countries and in many periods, civic activity won prestige because it attracted people of great worth and because its negative aspects did not seem to win out over the idealism, honesty and sense of responsibility of the majority of the political class. In our era those negative aspects of political life have often been magnified in an exaggerated and irresponsible way by the gutter press, with the result that public opinion has become convinced that politics is an activity full of amoral, inefficient and corruptible people.

The advances in audio-visual technology and the communications media, which help to counterbalance the systems of censorship and control in authoritarian societies, should have consolidated democracy and encouraged participation in public life. But it has rather had the opposite effect because the critical function of journalism has in many cases been distorted by the frivolity and the thirst for entertainment of the dominant culture. By exposing to the public, as Julian Assange's Wikileaks has done, the inner workings of political and diplomatic life in all its petty details and misfortunes, journalism has helped to strip any sense of respectability and seriousness from a profession that, in the past, preserved a certain mythic aura, as a fertile space for civilian heroism and daring initiatives in support of human rights, social justice, progress and freedom. The frantic search for scandal and cheap gossip with which to launch attacks on politicians has meant that, in many democracies, what the public knows about its politicians are their worst features. And these worst features normally chime with the very same lamentable behaviour that our civilization has imposed on everything that it touches: everything is a puppet show that can use very cheap tricks to win the favour of a public greedy for entertainment.

This is not a problem because problems have solutions and this does not. It is a reality of the civilization of our time, from which there is no way out. In theory, the law should fix the limits where information stops being in the public interest and infringes a citizen's right to privacy. But in most countries such a ruling is available only to stars and millionaires. No ordinary citizen can risk a court hearing that might drown him or her in a legal swamp and also cost a great deal of money if the judgment goes against him or her. And furthermore judges, with good reason, are often wary of handing down judgments that might seem to restrict or do away with freedom of expression and information, which is a guarantee of democracy.

Muckraking journalism is a perverse stepchild of the culture of freedom. We cannot curtail it without dealing freedom of expression a mortal blow. Since the cure would be worse than the illness, we must put up with it, in the same way that people put up with tumours, knowing that trying to cut them out might be life-threatening. We have not reached this state of affairs because of the murky machinations of owners of newspapers or television channels who exploit the lowest instincts of people in a completely irresponsible way. This in an effect, not the cause.

We can see this in the United Kingdom, one of the most civilized countries on earth, where, until recently, there was a belief that politics maintained high ethical and civic standards, besmirched only by the occasional theft or dishonest dealings of isolated individuals. The scandal around the powerful figure of Rupert Murdoch, the owner of a communications empire, News Corporation, and the London newspaper *News of the World*, which Murdoch has been forced to close, despite its enormous popularity, because it was discovered that its journalists had been illegally tapping the phones of thousands of people, including members of the royal family and an abducted girl, to feed the scandalous gossip that was the secret of the newspaper's success, has shown how far a press of this kind can have a harmful effect on institutions and politicians. The *News of the World* had on its payroll high-ranking officers of Scotland Yard; it bribed officials and politicians and used private detectives to delve into the private lives of famous people. Its power was so great that ministers, civil servants and even prime ministers courted its editors and executives, fearful that the newspaper might besmirch them by tying them into some scandal that would affect their reputation and their future.

Of course it is good that all this has come out into the

open and let us hope that the law will impose appropriate sanctions on the guilty parties. But I doubt whether, with this lesson, the evil will be rooted out because these roots spread very deeply in all strata of society.

The root of all this is in the culture. Or rather, in the playful banality of the dominant culture, in which the supreme value now is to amuse oneself and amuse others, over and above any form of knowledge or ideals. People open a newspaper, go to the cinema, turn on the television or buy a book to have a good time, in the lightest sense of the term, not to torment themselves with worries, problems or doubts. Just to amuse themselves, to forget serious, deep, disquieting and difficult things and to indulge in light, pleasant, superficial, happy and sanely stupid pursuits. And is there anything more amusing than spying on other people's private lives, catching a minister or parliamentarian with his trousers down, finding out about the sexual antics of a judge, or observing those who pass themselves off as respectable and exemplary wallowing in the mire?

The sensationalist press does not corrupt anybody; it emerges corrupted by a culture that, instead of rejecting the gross invasions into people's private lives, demands these invasions, because sniffing around other people's dirt makes the days of punctilious office workers, bored professionals and tired housewives more bearable. Stupidity has become the ruling value of postmodern life, and politics is one of its main victims.

In the civilization of the spectacle, it is perhaps the

politicians who get the worst coverage in the media. And this is another reason why, in the world today, there are so few exemplary leaders and statesmen and women – such as Nelson Mandela or Aung San Suu Kyi – who merit universal admiration.

Another consequence of all this is how little, if at all, the majority of people react to levels of corruption in developed countries and in so-called developing countries, both authoritarian and democratic, that are at perhaps their highest levels in history. This snobbish, don't-give-a-damn culture dulls society to its civic and moral responsibilities, allowing it to become much more indulgent towards the errant behaviour and excesses of anyone occupying public office and holding any kind of power. Furthermore this moral laxity occurs when economic life has progressed to such an extent across the planet and has reached such a level of complexity that the supervision of power that any society can achieve is much more difficult than in the past. And things become worse if journalism abandons its role of auditing society and instead looks to entertain its readers, listeners and viewers with scandal and gossip. All this helps to foster a sense of tolerance or indifference towards immorality in the great majority of people.

In the last elections in Peru, the writer Jorge Eduardo Benavides was surprised when a taxi driver in Lima told him that he was going to vote for Keiko Fujimori, the daughter of the dictator serving a twenty-five-year prison sentence for robbery and murder. 'Aren't you worried that President Fujimori was a thief?' he asked the taxi driver. 'No,' he replied. 'Because Fujimori only stole his fair share the right amount.' His fair share! This expression sums up perfectly everything I am trying to explain. The most trustworthy evaluation of the money siphoned off by Alberto Fujimori and his strong man Vladimir Monesinos, in their ten years in power (1990–2000), made by the National Attorney's Office, is some $6 billion, of which Switzerland, the Grand Caymans and the United States have returned to Peru scarcely $184 million. It was not just the taxi driver who thought that this scale of theft was acceptable because, although the daughter of the dictator lost the elections in 2011, she was on the point of winning: Ollanta Humala defeated her with the small difference of three percentage points.

Nothing demoralizes a society or discredits its institutions as much as the fact that its leaders, elected in more or less clean circumstances, take advantage of power in order to become rich, thus making a mockery of the trust the electorate puts in them. In Latin America – and in other regions of the world, of course – the main element in the growing criminality within public life has been the drugs trade. This is an industry that has witnessed modernization and an incredible growth since it has been able, like no other industry, to use globalization to extend its networks beyond borders, diversify, metamorphose, and recycle itself as a legal enterprise. Its enormous profits have allowed it to infiltrate all sectors of the state. Since it can pay better salaries than the state, it can buy, or bribe, judges, members of parliament, ministers, the police, judges and officials, or it can carry out intimidation and blackmail that almost guarantee its impunity. Rarely a day goes by without the discovery, in one or other country in Latin America, of another case of corruption linked to the drugs trade. Instead of provoking a critical response and a desire to combat this state of affairs, contemporary culture greets this situation with resignation and fatalism, in the same way that it responds to natural phenomena such as earthquakes and tsunamis, and sees it as a show, albeit a tragic and bloody one, that stirs strong emotions and emulsifies everyday life.

Of course culture cannot be held solely responsible for the devaluation of politics and the nature of public office. Another reason why the best professionals and managers steer clear of political life is because public office is usually badly paid. There is virtually nowhere in the world where salaries in a public sector are comparable to what a young person with good credentials and talent can eventually earn in a private company. Curbing the salaries of public employees is something that usually receives public approval, especially when the image of the state sector is at rock bottom, but the effects are prejudicial for the country in question. These low salaries are an incentive for corruption. And they put off the best-trained and most honest citizens from applying to public organizations, which means that these posts are often filled by incompetents and people of low moral standing.

For a democracy to function well it is essential to have a capable and honest civil service, like those which, in the past, laid the foundations for the greatness of France, the United Kingdom and Japan, to mention just three exemplary cases. In each of these countries, until relatively recently, serving the state was a prized job, since it merited respect as an honourable undertaking that contributed to the progress of the nation. These civil servants, in the main, received decent salaries and some degree of security as to their future. Although many of them could have earned more in private companies, they preferred public service, because what they might have lost in monetary terms was compensated by the fact that the work they were doing made them feel respected, because their fellow citizens understood the importance of their endeavours. In our era all this has almost completely disappeared. Civil servants are as discredited as professional politicians and public opinion tends to view them not as playing important roles but rather as hindrances and a drain on the public purse. Of course, bureaucratic inflation, the irresponsible growth in the number of civil servants as a way of paying political favours and creating a loyal clientelist base has sometimes turned public administration into a labyrinth in which the smallest transaction can become a nightmare for citizens who have no influence and cannot, or do not want to, pay bribes.

But it is wrong to generalize and place everyone in the same basket when there are many who resist such apathy and pessimism and show, with their discreet heroism, that democracy really does work.

There is a belief as widespread as it is unjust that corruption is undermining liberal democracies, that it will eventually achieve what defunct communism never managed: to bring about their collapse. Are there not daily discoveries, in old and in more recent democracies, of sickening cases where politicians and government employees have used political power to make fortunes at lightning speed? Are there not innumerable cases of judges being bribed, ill-gotten contracts, economic empires that have on their payroll soldiers, the police, ministers, and customs officials? Is not the system now so putrid that the only response is resignation, accepting that society is, and will always be, a jungle where the wild beasts will always devour the lambs?

It is not extensive corruption but rather this cynical, pessimistic attitude that might in effect bring an end to liberal democracies, turning them into a husk emptied of substance and truth, akin to what Marxists hold up to ridicule as 'formal' democracy. It is an attitude that is often unconscious, that takes the form of lack of interest and apathy towards public life, scepticism towards institutions and a reluctance to put them to the test. When considerable sections of a society feel that nothing is of consequence and resort to doom-watching and civic anomie, then the ground is clear for the wolves and hyenas.

It is not written in stone that all this will happen. The democratic system does not guarantee that dishonesty and cunning will disappear from human relations; but it does establish certain mechanisms to lessen the havoc, to detect, denounce and sanction people that use such improper means to rise up the ladder or become rich, and, most important of all, to reform the system in such a way that these crimes become ever more risky for those that commit them.

There is no democracy in our day and age in which new generations aspire to serve the state with the same enthusiasm with which, up till recently, the young idealists of the Third World dedicated themselves to revolutionary activity. This commitment saw hundreds of young men and women take to the mountains and jungles throughout most of Latin America in the 1960s and 1970s, convinced that socialist revolution was an ideal worth the sacrifice of their lives. They were wrong to think that communism was preferable to democracy, of course, but we cannot deny that they behaved in accordance with an ideal. In other regions of the world, such as Afghanistan, Pakistan or Iraq, young people imbued with Islamic fundamentalism offer up their lives today as human bombs, taking dozens of innocent lives in markets, on buses and in offices, convinced that these sacrifices will purify the world of sacrilegious and concupiscent people and crusaders. Of course such terrorist madness merits our condemnation and repudiation. But does not what occurred in the Arab Spring of 2011 make us at least a little enthusiastic once again, showing us that the culture of freedom is alive and is capable of radically changing history in a region where that seemed nigh on impossible?

The uprising of the Arab peoples against the satraps who exploited them and kept them in darkness has already deposed three tyrants, the Egyptian Hosni Mubarak, the Tunisian Zine al-Abidine Ben Ali and the Libyan Muammar al-Gaddafi. All the other authoritarian regimes of the region, starting with Syria, find themselves threatened by this awakening of millions of men and women who seek to escape authoritarianism, censorship and the plundering of wealth, to find work and live without fear, in peace and freedom, and embracing modernity.

This is a generous, idealistic, anti-authoritarian, popular and profoundly democratic movement. It has its roots in secular and civil society and had not been led or captured by fundamentalist sectors – not yet, at least – who would look to replace military dictatorships with religious dictatorships. In order to avoid this it is fundamental that Western democracies show solidarity and active support to those who today throughout the Middle East are fighting and dying for the right to live in freedom.[1]

---

1 December 2013. Unfortunately, in the case of many Arab countries my optimism – when I wrote these paragraphs in October 2011 – was excessive. For example, the Syrian rebellion against the tyranny of Bashar al-Assad has been distorted by the extremist and fanatical infiltration of Al Qaeda, while in Egypt, the sectarian excesses of the Muslim Brotherhood opened the doors of power once again to the army and allowed the re-establishment of an authoritarian military regime. In any event, the Popular Movement has not disappeared and has created significant momentum in countries such as Tunisia and Libya, which, despite the problems they face, are better off than under the dictatorships that the Popular Movement overthrew.

Now, faced with what is happening there, we might ask: how many young people in the West would today be prepared to face martyrdom for democratic culture, as the Libyans, the Tunisians, the Egyptians, the Yemeni, the Syrians and others have done and continue to do? How many who enjoy the privilege of living in open societies, supported by a rule of law, would risk their lives in defence of this type of society? Very few, for the simple reason that democratic and liberal society, despite having created the highest living standards in history and reduced social violence, exploitation and discrimination more than at any other time, does not receive the enthusiastic support of its beneficiaries, but is greeted with boredom and scorn, if not systematic hostility.

For example, let's consider artists and intellectuals. I began to write these lines at a time when, under the Cuban dictatorship, a dissident, Orlando Zapata, had let himself die after eighty-five days on hunger strike, protesting against the condition of political prisoners on the island, while another, Guillermo Fariñas, was dying after several weeks without food.[2] I also read in the Spanish press that an actor and a singer, both famous, are insulting them in the press, repeating the slogans of the Caribbean dictatorship and calling them 'delinquents'. Neither of them saw the difference between Cuba and Spain in terms of political repression and lack of freedom. How can we explain these attitudes? Fanaticism?

2 December 2013. Fortunately, he survived.

Ignorance? Mere stupidity? No. Frivolity. The buffoons and the comedians, who have become the *maîtres à penser* of contemporary society, speak the way they act: nothing strange about that. Their opinions purport to adhere to supposedly progressive ideas but, in reality, they merely repeat a snobbish left-wing script: stirring up trouble, giving people something to gossip about.

It is not bad that the main beneficiaries of freedom criticize open societies, where there is much that can be criticized. It is bad if they do so by taking the side of those who seek to destroy these open societies, replacing them with authoritarian regimes, as in Venezuela or Cuba. When many artists and intellectuals betray democratic ideals, they are not betraying abstract principles, but rather the thousands and millions of flesh-and-blood people who, under dictatorships, resist and fight to gain freedom. But the saddest thing is that this betrayal of the victims does not come from principles and convictions but rather from professional opportunism and posturing, gestures and actions adapted to circumstance. Many artists and intellectuals in our times have become very cheap.

A key feature of our age that helps to weaken democracy is indifference towards the law, another of the grave consequences of the civilization of the spectacle.

Let's be clear, we must not confuse this careless indifference towards the law with the rebellious or revolutionary attitudes of those who seek to destroy the existing legal structure because they consider it intolerable and look to replace it with another more equitable and just system. Indifference to the law has nothing to do with this reformist or revolutionary desire, with its hope for change and for a better society. These attitudes have almost been extinguished in today's culture following the great failure of the communist experiment, whose fate was sealed by the fall of the Berlin Wall, the disappearance of the Soviet Union and the conversion of People's China into a country with a capitalist economy but with a vertical and authoritarian political structure. There are, of course, here and there, heirs to the broken utopia, but these are minority groups and groupuscules that have little chance of survival. The last communist countries on the planet, Cuba and North Korea, are living anachronisms, museum pieces that cannot offer a model to anyone. And the Venezuela of Comandante Hugo Chávez, and his successor Nicolás Maduro, which is struggling, despite its copious oil reserves, with an unprecedented economic crisis, would not be the best example of how to revive the communist model that in the 1960s and 1970s was enthusiastically embraced by large numbers in the First and Third Worlds.

Indifference to the law has grown up within democratic societies and with it an attitude of contempt or disdain for existing legal regimes alongside a moral indifference and anomie that permits citizens to flout the law as often as they can, to gain from this – usually financially – but also, often, simply to show their contempt, incredulity or mockery of the existing order. People, at least some people in this era of civilization as entertainment, break the law to amuse themselves, as if they were practising a risky sport.

One explanation for this indifference to the law is that often laws are badly made, that they are dictated not to benefit the common good but to benefit particular interests, or they are framed so clumsily that citizens feel obliged to get around them. It is obvious that if a government weighs taxpayers down with inappropriately severe taxes, then they will be tempted to evade their financial obligations. Bad laws work not just against the interests of ordinary citizens; they also bring the legal system into disrepute and encourage this indifference that, like a poison, eats away at democracy. There have always been bad governments just as there have always been ridiculous or unjust laws. But, in a democratic society, unlike in a dictatorship, there are ways of denouncing, opposing and correcting these abuses by participating in the system, using the freedom of the press, the right to criticize, independent journalism, opposition parties, elections, the mobilization of public opinion, and, of course, law courts. But for this to work it is essential that the democratic system has the confidence and support of its citizens, and that, no matter what its shortcomings, it is a system that is seen to be open to improvement. Indifference to the law is a result of the collapse in this confidence, a feeling that it is the system itself that is rotten and that bad laws are not exceptions but an inevitable consequence of the corruption and deals that are integral to the system. One of the direct consequences of the devaluation of politics in the civilization of the spectacle is indifference towards the law.

I remember one of the strongest impressions that I had when I went to live in England in 1966 – I had spent the previous seven years in France – was to discover this respect, one might almost call it natural, at once spontaneous, instinctive and rational, for the law among ordinary British people. The explanation seemed to be the deeply rooted belief that, in general, laws were well conceived, that they were geared to the common good, and, for this reason, they had a *moral* legitimacy: therefore, what the law authorized was right and good and what the law prohibited was wrong and bad. This surprised me because in the places I had lived in before, Peru, Bolivia and France, I had never witnessed anything similar. This identification of law with morality is an Anglo-Saxon and Protestant characteristic, and is not usually a feature of Latin or Hispanic countries. In these countries, citizens tend to be resigned to the law rather than seeing it as embodying moral and religious principles, and to consider the law as a body that is alien (not necessarily hostile or antagonistic) to their spiritual beliefs.

In any event, if this distinction was true in the neighbourhoods where I lived in London, it is probably not as true today, when, partly as a result of globalization, indifference to the law is a common feature of Anglo-Saxon, Latin and Hispanic countries. This indifference presupposes that laws are the work of a power that is merely self-serving, that is, which serves the people who embody and administer power, and that, therefore, the resulting laws, rules and regulations are riddled with self-ishness and individual and group special interests, which absolves the run-of-the-mill citizen from obeying them. Most people adhere to the law because there is no other alternative, out of fear, that is, perceiving that it would be more damaging than beneficial to try to transgress the rules, but this attitude is as damaging to the legitimacy and strength of a legal regime as is openly law-breaking. This means that, when it comes to obeying the law, con-temporary civilization treats it as a sham, a sham that, in many places, and quite often, degenerates into mere farce.

There is no better example of this general indifference to the law today than the widespread piracy of books, records, DVDs and other audiovisual products, mainly music, which has become widespread throughout every country on earth, with few obstacles and, one might say, even with general approval.

In Peru, for example, the piracy of videos and films bankrupted the Blockbuster chain, and from that moment people who like watching movies on their televisions have not been able to get hold of legal DVDs, even if they want to, because they scarcely exist in the market, outside a few stores, which import some titles and sell them at very high prices. The entire country stocks up on pirated films, mainly in the extraordinary Lima market in Polvos Azules where, in plain view of the world – including the police who protect the place against robbery – thousands of pirated DVDs are sold every day very cheaply, classic and modern films, many of which have not even yet reached the city's cinemas. The pirate industry is so efficient that if customers do not find the movies they want, they order them and have a copy in their hands within a few days. I mention Polvos Azules because the place is so vast and is so commercially successful. It has become a tourist attraction. There are people who come from Chile and Argentina to Lima to restock their video libraries. But this market is not the only place where piracy prospers openly, with general support. Who would not buy pirated films for half a dollar if the legal films (which are mostly not available) cost five times as much? Sellers of pirated DVDs are now everywhere and I know people who place orders over the phone because there is also a home delivery service. Those of us who do not go along with buying pirated films as a point of principle are a tiny handful of people, and we are considered (not without reason) idiots.

What is happening with DVDs also happens with books. Book piracy has prospered quite significantly, especially in the underdeveloped world, and the campaigns against this waged by publishers and national Book Chambers, set up to support publishers and writers, usually fail resoundingly due to the lack of support that they receive from governments and, above all, from the general public, who have no scruples about buying illegal books, justifying their actions by the low cost of the pirated version compared to the genuine book. In Lima, a writer, critic and university professor made a public statement in praise of book piracy, saying that by this means books reached the people. The effect of piracy on publishers, on authors, and on the state, which receives no tax revenue on pirated books, is not taken into account by anybody for the simple reason that there is a general indifference towards the law. Publishing piracy began as an artisanal industry but, thanks to the impunity that it enjoys, it has developed to such a level of industrial sophistication that in countries such as Peru what has happened with DVDs might well happen with books: the pirates might bankrupt the legal publishers and take over the market. Alfaguara, my publisher, calculates that for every legitimate sale of my books in Peru, there are six or seven pirated sales. (One of the pirated versions of my novel *The Feast of the Goat* was published by the army's publishing house!)

But music is an even worse case than films or books. Not only due to the proliferation of pirate CDs, but also thanks to the ease and total impunity with which Internet users can download songs, concerts and records from the net. All the campaigns to stop music piracy have proved ineffective and, as a result, many music outlets have collapsed or are facing ruin due to this unfair competition, which the public connives at, in ever-increasing numbers.

The threat to the integrity of films, records, books and music is replicated, of course, in the case of any number of manufactured goods. In Rome, I once had to go with some tourist friends to a vast 'fakes market' (pirated clothes and shoes from designer brands), which, with designer labels in place, were being sold at a quarter or a fifth of the price of the genuine articles. So this indifference to the law is not just the domain of the Third World. Even in the First World it is beginning to wreak havoc, threatening the survival of industries and stores that operate within the law.

Our remarks on this widespread indifference to the law lead us inevitably to consider in the next chapter a more spiritual dimension of life in society. The great loss of prestige of politics is doubtless related to the break-up of the spiritual order that, in the past, at least in the Western world, could curb the outbursts and excesses committed by the powerful. Since that spiritual tutelage disappeared from public life, all manner of demons have prospered that have degraded politics and induced people to see politics not as something noble and altruistic, but rather as a largely dishonest activity. Culture should fill the void that was previously occupied by religion. But it is impossible for this to happen if culture, betraying this responsibility, is resolutely geared towards simplicity, shies away from the most urgent human problems, and becomes mere entertainment.

PRIVATE AND PUBLIC

El País, Madrid, 16 January 2011

Ever since I began reading his books and articles – it must have been about thirty years ago – I've found that something happens to me with Fernando Savater that does not occur with any other of my favourite writers: I almost never disagree with his opinions and his critiques. His arguments, generally, convince me immediately, even if that means that I have to revise radically what I had previously thought.

Whether he is talking about politics, literature, ethics and even about horses (which I know nothing about, except that I never won a single bet the very few times I went to a track), Savater has always seemed to me a model of the committed intellectual, both principled and pragmatic, one of those rare contemporary thinkers with the ability to see clearly in the complex wood that is this twenty-first century and to help those of us who are wandering somewhat lost to find the missing path.

I was reminded of this when I read an article of his on WikiLeaks and Julian Assange in *Tiempo* magazine (23 December 2010–6 January 2011). I would strongly urge everyone who has celebrated the publishing of thousands of confidential US State Department documents as a heroic act of freedom to read this article, which is brimming with intelligence, courage and good sense. If it does not make them change their opinion, then it is sure at least to make them consider and question whether their enthusiasm was not somewhat hasty.

Savater shows that in this vast collection of leaked material there are practically no important revelations, that the information and confidential opinions that have come to light were already known or deducible by any more or less informed observer of contemporary politics, and that what makes up the bulk of the material is mainly gossip aimed at appealing to a frivolity that, under the respectable heading of transparency, is really the established 'right of everyone to know everything: for there should be no secrets or reservations standing in the way of someone's curiosity . . . whatever might happen and whatever we might lose on the way.' This presumed 'right' is, he adds, 'part of the current dumbing down of society'. I subscribe to this statement wholeheartedly.

The audio-visual revolution of our times has broken through the barriers that censorship erected to curb freedom of information and critical dissent and, thanks to this, authoritarian regimes now have many fewer possibilities than in the past to keep their nations in ignorance and to manipulate public opinion. This, of course, is a great advance for the culture of freedom and one should make use of it. But to go further and argue that the prodigious transformations brought about by the Internet authorize Internet users to know everything and divulge everything that happens under the sun, dissolving once and for all the demarcation between public and private, is to take a giant leap that might not be an act of freedom but rather an assault on freedom itself, which would undermine the foundations of democracy and deal a rude blow to civilization.

No democracy could function if the confidentiality of communications between employees and the authorities were to disappear, nor could there be any consistency in any policy in the fields of diplomacy, defence, security, public order and even the economy if the processes that determine these policies were, at every stage, exposed to the public gaze. The result of such information exhibitionism would be the paralysis of institutions and would help antidemocratic organizations to hamper and thwart any initiatives at variance with their authoritarian designs. Information licentiousness is not the same as freedom of expression; it is the opposite.

Such licentiousness is possible only in open societies, not in those subject to vertical police control, which severely punishes any attempt to break through censorship. It is not accidental that the two hundred and fifty thousand confidential documents that WikiLeaks has obtained come from sources in the United States, not in Russia or China. Although the intentions of Julian Assange chime with the utopian and anarchist dream of total transparency, his attempts to put an end to 'secrecy' might more likely lead us to a situation in which certain forces, using the justification that confidentiality must be maintained within the state, could impose restrictions and limitations on one of the most important rights of democratic life: the right to freedom of expression and to criticize.

In a free society, government action is overseen by parliament or congress, the courts, independent and opposition press, political parties, and other institutions that have every right in the world to denounce the deceits and lies that some states engage in to cover up illegal actions or deals. But what WikiLeaks has done is nothing like that; instead it has brutally destroyed the privacy of communications in which diplomats tell their superiors about the private political, economic, cultural and social affairs of the countries where they are based. A lot of this material is made up of pieces of information and commentaries that, if widely circulated, would not be of much importance, but could certainly create very delicate situations for those civil servants and lead to grudges and resentments that could only damage relations between allied countries and discredit their governments. It is not therefore about fighting against a 'lie', but rather about satisfying this morbid and unhealthy curiosity of the civilization of the spectacle, the civilization of our age, where journalism (like culture in general) is guided by the need to entertain. Julian Assange, rather than being a great freedom fighter, is a successful entertainer, the Oprah Winfrey of the information world.

If he had not existed, our era would have created him sooner or later, because this character is the emblematic symbol of a culture where the supreme value of information has become that of amusing a foolish and superficial public thirst for scandals that delve into the private lives of famous people, showing their weaknesses and their entanglements, turning them into the clowns of the great farce that is public life – although, perhaps, it is now inaccurate to talk of a 'public life' because that presupposes a 'private life', something that has gradually disappeared and has now become an empty and obsolete category.

What is private today? One of the involuntary consequences of the information revolution is to have
destroyed the borders that separated it from the public
arena. And to have blended both into a 'happening' in
which we are all both spectators and actors, in which we
can, reciprocally, show off our private lives and amuse
ourselves observing the private lives of others in a universal striptease where nobody is any longer spared
morbid public curiosity.

The disappearance of what is private, where nobody
respects the privacy of others, where privacy has become
a parody that excites general interest and where there is an
information industry that feeds incessantly on this universal voyeurism, is a manifestation of barbarism. Because,
with the disappearance of the realm of the private, many of
the best achievements of humanity deteriorate and become
degraded, beginning with everything that has safeguarded
certain forms including eroticism, love, friendship, modesty, good manners, art and morality.

If governments elected in legal ballots can be overthrown by revolutions that seek to bring paradise to
earth (though often they bring hell), well, so be it. Or if
conflicts and even bloody wars arise between countries
defending incompatible religions, ideologies or ambitions, this is a pity. But if such tragedies might occur
because our privileged contemporaries have got bored
and need strong entertainment, and an Internet dowser
such as Julian Assange gives them what they want, that
would be an ultimate reduction to absurdity.

VI

The Opium of the People

Contrary to what the freethinkers, agnostics and atheists of the nineteenth and twentieth centuries imagined, in the postmodern era religion is not dead and buried; nor has it been dispatched to the attic where useless things accumulate: it is alive and kicking, at the centre of today's debates.

There is no way of knowing, of course, if the fervour of believers and practising members of the different religions that exist in the world has increased or decreased. But no one can deny the presence of religion in contemporary social, political and cultural life. It is probably as strong, or even stronger, than it was in the nineteenth century, when intellectual and civic struggles for and against secularism preoccupied many countries on both sides of the Atlantic.

A central protagonist of contemporary politics, the suicide terrorist, who is viscerally linked to religion, is a by-product of the most fundamentalist and fanatical version of Islamism. The struggle of Al Qaeda and its leader, the late Osama bin Laden, is, above all religious, a purifying offensive against bad Muslims and Islamist renegades as well as against the infidels, Nazarenes (Christians) and degenerates of the West, led by the Great Satan, the United States. In the Arab world, the confrontation that

has generated the most violence is unequivocally religious, and Islamist terrorism has claimed more victims
among the Muslim population than among believers
from other religions, if we take into account the number
of Iraqis killed or maimed by Shia and Sunni extremist
groups, and the killing in Afghanistan by the Taliban, a
fundamentalist movement that was born in the *madrasas*,
Afghan and Pakistani religious schools, and which, like
Al Qaeda, has never hesitated to kill Muslims who do not
share their fundamentalist puritanism.

The divisions and conflicts in Muslim societies have
not helped in any way to lessen the influence of religion
in people's lives; rather, they have exacerbated this influence. Secularism has not gained any ground. Secular
groups have shrunk in recent years with the growth in
the Lebanon of Hezbollah ('God's Party') and in Palestine of Hamas, which gained control of the Gaza Strip in
open elections. And in the first free elections in Tunisia
and Egypt in their entire history, the majority of votes
was cast in favour of Islamist parties (though for the
most part moderate groups).

If this is happening in the heart of Islam, we cannot
claim that coexistence between the different Christian
denominations, churches and sects is always peaceful.
In Northern Ireland, the struggle between the Protestant majority and the Catholic minority, now ended
(hopefully for ever), has left a large number of dead and
injured through the criminal actions of the extremists
on both sides.

Catholicism is also riven by great conflicts at its very core. Some years ago the most intense of these was between traditionalists and progressives who supported Liberation Theology, a dispute that seems to have been resolved for the moment, following the election of two conservative popes – John Paul II and Benedict XVI – with the curbing (but not the defeat) of the progressives.[1]

The most acute problem facing the Catholic Church has been the revelation of a significant tradition of rape and paedophilia in schools, seminaries, children's homes and parishes, a horrifying reality that had been hinted at years ago, but any suspicion of which the Church managed to silence for a long time. But in recent years, thanks to the actions of the victims themselves, often going through the courts, these cases of sexual abuse have been coming out in the open in such numbers that one cannot speak of isolated cases, but rather of widespread practices ranging over time and space in many countries. This fact has caused disgust across the world, especially among the faithful themselves. The testimonies of thousands of victims in almost all Catholic countries has taken the Church in places such as Ireland and the United States to the verge of bankruptcy because of the huge amount of money that it has been forced to spend defending itself in court or paying damages and compensation to the victims of rape and sexual abuse committed by priests.

1 December 2013. The resignation of Benedict XVI and the election to the Throne of Saint Peter of Pope Francis has raised great hopes for renovation and modernization within the Catholic Church.

Despite its protestations, it is clear that at least part of the ecclesiastical hierarchy – the accusations extended to the highest echelons of the papacy – were complicit with these paedophiles, protecting them, not reporting them to the authorities, and merely changing their postings, and allowing them to continue with priestly duties, including teaching children. The strong condemnation by Pope Benedict XVI of the Legionaries of Christ, which he had ordered to be reorganized root and branch, and of its founder, the Mexican Father Marcial Maciel, a bigamist, a committer of incest, a fraudster, a rapist of boys and girls, including one of his own children – a character seemingly escaped from the novels of the Marquis de Sade – has not dispersed the shadows that such scandals have thrown over one of the most important religions in the world.

Has all this scandal lessened the influence of the Catholic Church? I would not dare to say yes. It is true that in many countries seminaries are closing through a lack of novices, and that, compared with the past, the alms, donations, bequests and legacies that the Church receives have declined. But despite financial losses, such difficulties seem to have sharpened the resolve and the engagement of Catholics who have never before been so active in social campaigns, demonstrating against gay marriage, the legalization of abortion, contraception, euthanasia and secularism. In countries such as Spain this mass mobilization of Catholics is very wide-ranging and at times is so virulent that one could not consider the Church as in any way on the ropes. The political and social power that the Church exerts in most Latin American countries remains undiminished, which is why, when it comes to sexual freedom and women's liberation, progress has been minimal. In most Hispanic American countries the Catholic Church has managed to make the pill and the morning-after pill illegal, along with all other forms of contraception. This ban, of course, is effective only for poor women because middle- and upper-class women make extensive use of contraceptive methods and abortion despite the legal prohibition.

Something similar can be said of Protestant churches. They have sought in the United States to make school education chime with the teachings of the Bible, and have Darwin's theory of the evolution of the species banned from the curriculum, having it replaced, instead, by 'creationism' or 'intelligent design', an anti-scientific teaching that, however anachronistic and obscurantist it might appear, could well be adopted in some North American states where religious influence is very strong in politics.

Furthermore, the Protestant missionary offensive in Latin America and in other Third World regions is enormous, resolute and has achieved notable success. In many extremely poor, isolated and marginal areas, the Evangelical churches have displaced Catholicism, which, because of its lack of priests or a decline in missionary zeal, has given ground to the energetic Protestant sects. They are often welcomed by women, thanks to their ban on alcohol and their demand that new converts should constantly observe religious practices, something that helps family stability and keeps husbands away from bars and brothels.

The truth is that in almost all the bloodiest conflicts in recent years – Israel–Palestine, the Balkan war, the violence in Chechnya, the incidents in China in the region of Xinjiang, where there have been uprisings of the Muslim Uyghurs, the killings of Hindus and Muslims in India, the conflicts between India and Pakistan, etc. – religion lies at the heart of the conflict and of the social divisions that lead to bloodshed. The case of the Soviet Union and its satellite countries is instructive. With the fall of communism, after sixty years of persecuting churches and advocating atheism, not only has religion not disappeared; it has been reborn and once again plays a prominent role in society. In Russia the churches are once again full and Orthodox priests have reappeared officially, and the same is true in Slavic societies that were formerly under Soviet control. Religion, Orthodox or Catholic, never disappeared but remained dormant and out of sight to guard against attack, always relying on the discreet support of vast sectors of society. The rebirth of the Russian Orthodox Church is impressive. Successive governments under Putin and under Medvedev have begun to return the church buildings and religious properties confiscated by the Bolsheviks and there is even a move to return the cathedrals of the Kremlin, along with the monasteries, the schools, the works of art and the cemeteries that formerly belonged to the Church. It is estimated that since the fall of communism the number of the Orthodox faithful has tripled throughout Russia.

Religion, then, shows no signs of disappearing. Everything indicates that it will be around for some time yet. Is this good or bad for culture and for freedom?

The reply to this question offered by the British scientist Richard Dawkins, who has published a book against religion and in defence of atheism – *The God Delusion* – and by the journalist and essayist Christopher Hitchens, the author of *God Is Not Great: The Case Against Religion*, leaves no room for doubt. But in this polemic, in which these two writers have played a leading role, reviving the old charges of obscurantism, superstition, irrationality, gender discrimination, authoritarianism and retrograde conservatism levelled against religions, there have been also some scientists, including the Nobel Prize winner for physics, Charles Tornes (who backs the theory of 'intelligent design'), who defend, with no less enthusiasm, their religious beliefs and refute the arguments that faith in God and practising religion are incompatible with modernity, progress, freedom and the discoveries and truths of contemporary science.

This is not a polemic that can be won or lost with reasoned arguments because there is always a *parti pris* that precedes such arguments: an act of faith. There is no way of demonstrating rationally whether God exists or not. Any reasoning in favour of a theory can be countered by an opposing theory, so that any analysis or discussion on this matter that wants to stay within the confines of reason must begin by excluding any metaphysical or theological premise – the existence or non-existence of God – and concentrate on the consequences and effects derived from such premises: the function of churches and religions in the historical development and cultural life of societies, something that is certainly verifiable through human reason.

A fundamental fact to bear in mind is that belief in a supreme being, and in a life that precedes and follows life on earth, forms part of every known culture and civilization. There are no exceptions to this rule. They all have their god or gods and all trust in another life after death, although what that transcendent life might be is infinitely variable according to time and place. How can we explain why human beings from every time and place have espoused this belief? Atheists reply immediately: this is due to ignorance and a fear of death. Men and women, irrespective of their level of knowledge or culture, from the most primitive to the most refined, cannot accept the idea of definitive extinction, that their existence is a passing and accidental fact and, for that reason, need there to be another life, presided over by a supreme being. The greater the level of ignorance of a community, the greater is the strength of religion. When scientific knowledge clears away the fuzziness and the superstitions from the human mind and replaces them with objective truths, then the entire artificial construction of cults and beliefs with which the primitive mind seeks to explain the world, nature and the afterlife, begins to crack. This is the beginning of the end for the magical and irrational interpretation of life and death, which will, in the end, make religion fade and disappear.

That is the theory. In practice this has not happened and does not show any signs of happening. The development of scientific and technological knowledge has been prodigious (not always benign) since the time of the cave dwellers and has allowed human beings to gain a profound knowledge of nature, outer space, their own bodies, to discover their past, wage decisive battles against disease and raise the living standards of people to a degree unimaginable to our ancestors. But, apart from the case of relatively small minorities in some societies and a majority in few others, it has not managed to wrench God from the heart of men and women, or to do away with religions. The argument of the atheists is that this is still an ongoing process, that the advance of science has not stopped, it is still progressing, and that sooner or later there will be an end to this atavistic struggle and that God and religion will disappear, banished from human existence by scientific truths. This article of faith for nineteenth-century liberals and progressive thinkers is difficult to defend in today's world, which offers ample proof to the contrary: God surrounds us on all sides and, disguised in political garb, religious wars continue to cause the same havoc to humanity as in medieval times. This does not demonstrate that God really does exist, but rather that the vast majority of people, including many prominent specialists and scientists, are not prepared to give up a divinity that guarantees them some form of survival after death.

Furthermore it is not just the idea of death, of physical extinction, that has kept notions of transcendence alive throughout history. There is also the complementary belief that, for this life to be bearable, it is necessary, indeed indispensable, that there should be an authority higher than earthly authority, where good is rewarded and evil is punished, which can distinguish between good and bad actions, make good the injustices and cruelties that we suffer and punish those who inflict them on us. The reality is that, despite all the judicial advances that have been made in society since ancient times, there is no human community in existence in which the bulk of the population does not have the feeling that total justice is not possible in this world. They all believe, no matter how fair the law is, or how respectable the judges commissioned to administer it, or how honourable and decent the system of government might be, that justice never manages to be a tangible reality, within everyone's reach, something that will defend ordinary individuals, anonymous citizens, from being abused, trampled on and discriminated against by those in power. So it is not unusual to find religion and religious practices more deeply rooted among the more disadvantaged classes of society, those who, due to their poverty and vulnerability, are the targets of abuses and ill-treatment of all kinds, which usually go unpunished. One can put up with poverty, discrimination, exploitation and abuse better if one believes that posthumous amends will be made for all this. (This is why Marx called religion 'the opium of the people', a drug that anaesthetized the rebellious spirit of the workers and allowed their masters to carry on blithely exploiting them.)

Another reason why human beings cling to the idea of an all-powerful god and an afterlife is that so many of us suspect that if this idea were to disappear and instead it were established as an unequivocal scientific truth that God does not exist, then, sooner or later, social life would become barbaric, there would be a return to the law of the jungle and the rule of the strongest, and that society would be taken over by the most destructive and cruel tendencies that live within men and women, tendencies that are not curbed or moderated by human laws or by morality based on rational government, but rather by religion. In other words, if there is something that can still be called morality, a body of norms of behaviour that fosters good, coexistence within diversity, generosity, altruism, compassion, respect for one's neighbour, and rejects violence, abuse, theft, exploitation, then it can be found in religion, in divine law, not human laws. If this antidote were to disappear, life would gradually turn into a witches' sabbath of savagery, arrogance and excess where the controllers of any form of power – political, economic or military – would feel free to commit every possible form of abuse, giving free rein to their most destructive instincts and urges. If this life is the only one we have and there is nothing after it, and we will be dead for ever and ever, why don't we try to make the best possible use of it even though this might mean bringing about our own ruin and strewing the ground with the victims of our unleashed instincts? Men and women insist on believing in God because they do not trust themselves. And history shows us that they are right to think this because up until now we have not shown ourselves to be trustworthy.

This does not mean, of course, that the validity of religion can guarantee the triumph of good over evil in this world, or offer an effective morality to curb violence and cruelty in human relations. It just means that, however badly things might be going in the world, a vague instinct leads a greater part of humanity to believe that they would become even worse if atheists and extreme secularists were to achieve their objective of eradicating God and religion from our lives. This can only be an intuition or a belief (another act of faith): there are no statistics to prove the case, one way or the other.

There is one final reason, a philosophical or, more strictly speaking, a metaphysical reason, for this very prolonged attachment to God and religion in human consciousness. Contrary to what the freethinkers believed, neither scientific knowledge nor culture in general – much less a culture devastated by frivolity – are enough to release men and women from the solitude brought on by the premonition that there is no afterlife. It is not a fear of death, the horror at the prospect of total extinction, rather a feeling of abandonment and loss in this life, here and now, caused by the mere suspicion that there is no other life, there is no place beyond where a being or beings more powerful and wiser than humans know and determine the meaning of life, of temporal and historical order, that is, the meaning of the mystery of why we are born, live and die, beings whose wisdom we can understand in part, sufficient to make sense of and justify our own existence. Despite all the advances it has made, science has not been able to reveal this mystery, and it is unlikely that it will ever do so. Very few human beings are capable of accepting the idea of the 'existentialist absurd', that we are 'cast' here in the world through the workings of incomprehensible chance, a stellar accident, that our lives are mere chance without order or harmony, and that all that will happen in these lives is exclusively dependent on our behaviour and our will and on our social and historical circumstances. This idea, which Albert Camus described in *The Myth of Sisyphus* with great lucidity and serenity and drew elegant conclusions from it concerning beauty, freedom and pleasure, plunges most mortals into anomie, paralysis and desperation.

In the first essay in *El hombre y lo divino* (*Man and the Divine*), 'On the Birth of the Gods', María Zambrano asks, 'How were the gods born and why?' The answer that she gives predates and is more profound than the notion of primitive men and women becoming aware of their defencelessness, solitude and vulnerability. In fact, she says, it is an integral part of our make-up, a 'vast, distinctive need of the human condition' to feel, in the face of the world, a sense of 'unease' that springs from a 'persecution mania' that stops, or at least abates, only when we humans recognize and feel that we are surrounded by gods whose presence we previously intuited, and which had us living in anxiety and frenzy until we recognized them and incorporated them into our lives. Zambrano investigates the specific case of the Greek gods, but her conclusions apply to all civilizations and cultures. Were this not the case, she asks, 'Why have there always been gods, of different types, of course, but, in the final analysis, gods?' She gives the answer to this question in another essay in the book, 'The Tracks of Paradise', and it could not be more convincing: 'And in the two extremes that mark out the horizon of humanity, the lost past and the future to be created, there glows the desire and anxiety for a divine life which is also human, a divine life that man seems to have always had as an earlier model, that he has drawn from out of the confusion in bright images, like a shaft of pure light that takes on colour as it crosses the turbulent atmosphere of passions, of need and of suffering.'[2]

In the 1960s I lived in London, during a moment when a new culture was emerging forcefully and was spreading from there throughout most of the Western world: hippy culture, flower children. The most innovative and

2 María Zambrano, *El hombre y lo divino*, Opera Mundi, Barcelona, 1999, pp. 145–9 and 429.

distinctive aspects of the movement were the musical revolution that came with it (notably the Beatles and the Rolling Stones), a new style of dress, the use of marijuana and other drugs, sexual freedom but also the re-emergence of a religious sensibility that did not draw from the great traditional religions of the West, but instead looked towards the East, to Buddhism and Hinduism in particular and all the cults associated with them, as well as to innumerable sects and primitive religious practices, many of dubious origin and at times fabricated by second-rate gurus and colourful opportunists. But irrespective of how naive, modish and dilettantist aspects of this movement might appear, it is true that behind this proliferation of churches and exotic beliefs there were thousands of young people from across the world who became committed to them and brought their energy to them, and went on pilgrimage to Kathmandu as their grandfathers before them had visited the Holy Land or Muslims visited Mecca. They demonstrated in a very palpable way the need for spiritual life and transcendence that only small minorities in the course of history have managed to escape. It is instructive that so many nonconformists and rebels against the dominance of Christianity would later fall under the spell of the religious-psychedelic preaching of people such as the father of LSD, Timothy Leary; the Maharishi Mahesh Yogi, the holy man and favourite guru of the Beatles, or the Korean prophet of the Moonies and the Church of Unification, the Reverend Sun Myung Moon.

Not many people have taken seriously this revival of superficial religious sentiment, with its picturesque aspects, its naivety and its movie paraphernalia and the proliferation of cults and churches promoted by shrill, tasteless advertising as commercial products for domestic consumption. But the fact that they are of recent origin, at times grotesquely fraudulent, and that they take advantage of the lack of culture, naivety and frivolity of their followers, does not stop them offering a spiritual service to their followers, helping them to fill a void in their lives, as happens to millions of other human beings in the traditional churches. There is no other way of explaining why some of these recent churches, such as the Church of Scientology, founded by L. Ron Hubbard, which is favoured by some Hollywood luminaries such as Tom Cruise and John Travolta, have survived relentless investigation in countries including Germany, where the Church of Scientology was accused of brainwashing and exploiting minors, and have built up major international economic empires. It is not in any way surprising that in the civilization of the pantomime, religion becomes something of a circus and at times turns into a circus.

To take stock of the function of religions throughout human history, it is essential to separate the effects that they have in the private and individual sphere from that in the public and social sphere. One should not confuse the two because to do so would be to miss fundamental points and also different nuances. For believers, their religion – whether an old, deep-rooted and popular religion or one that is contemporary and superficial – gives them a form of solace. It allows them to explain to themselves who they are and what they are doing in this world; it gives them an order and a moral code by which to organize their lives and behaviour, gives them the hope of life after death, consolation for misfortune, and the relief and security derived from feeling part of a community with shared beliefs, rituals and lifestyles. Above all for those who suffer from, and are the victims of, abuse, exploitation, poverty, frustration and misfortune, religion is a form of salvation that they cling to so as not to give in to the desperation that might undermine their capacity to react to and resist misfortune, and drive them towards suicide.

From a social point of view there are also many positive consequences of religion. In the case of Christianity, for example, it was a revolution for its time to preach forgiveness, which included one's enemies, whom Christ taught should be loved along with one's friends, and to turn poverty into a moral value that God would reward in another life ('the last shall be first') as well as the condemnation of wealth and of the rich man that Jesus makes in St Mark's Gospel (10:24): 'It is easier for a camel to go through the eye of a needle than for a rich man to enter the kingdom of God.' Christianity proposed a universal fraternity, which would fight against prejudice and discrimination between races, cultures and ethnic groups and assert that they were all, without exception, the sons and daughters of God and were welcome in the House of the Lord. Although these ideas took time to become incorporated into state and government practices, they did help to alleviate the most brutal forms of exploitation, discrimination and violence and refine life in the old world as well as laying the foundations for what, over time, would be the recognition of human rights, the abolition of slavery, and the condemnation of genocide and torture. In other words, Christianity played a crucial role in the birth of democratic culture.

But while Christianity would serve democracy through the philosophy implicit in its doctrine, in societies that had not become secularized, it became one of the greatest obstacles preventing democracy from expanding and taking root. In this it was no different from any other religion. Religions accept and promulgate only absolute truths and every religion rejects the truths of other religions in a categorical manner. They all aspire not only to conquer the hearts and souls of human beings, but also to control their behaviour. While it was a catacomb religion, marginal, persecuted, a cult of the poor and the destitute, Christianity represented a form of civilization that contrasted with the barbarism of the pagans, their crazed violence, their prejudices and superstitions, the excesses of their lives and their inhumanity towards others. But when it took root and began incorporating the ruling classes into its fold, and began to co-govern society, or to govern it directly, then Christianity lost its image of tolerance. In power it became intolerant, dogmatic, exclusivist and fanatical. Defence of orthodoxy caused it to inflict similar or worse violence than that suffered by the first Christians at the hands of the pagans and to legitimate wars and iniquitous cruelties against its adversaries. The Church's identification with, or proximity to, power often caused it to make shameful concessions to kings, princes, caudillos and to the powerful in general. If in certain periods, such as the Renaissance, the Church favoured the development of arts and letters – Dante, Piero della Francesca and Michelangelo would not have been possible without this patronage – it would later become, in the realm of thought, brutally repressive, as it was in the domain of scientific research, censuring and punishing even with torture and death, thinkers, scientists and artists suspected of heterodoxy. The Crusades, the Inquisition, the Index are some of the symbols of the intransigence, the dogmatism and the ferocity with which the Church fought against intellectual, scientific and artistic freedom, and, by the same token, the great fighters for freedom in Catholic countries had to wage war against the Church. In Protestant countries there was less intolerance towards science and a less strict censorship of literature and the arts, but there was the same rigidity as in Catholic countries when it came to the family, sex and love. In both cases, discrimination against women found a champion in the Church and in both cases the churches encouraged or tolerated anti-Semitism.

Only with the development of secular society would the Church accept (or rather become resigned to) the fact of giving to Caesar what is Caesar's and to God what is God's. That is, to accept a strict division between the spiritual and the temporal, that they would have control in the spiritual realm while respecting what all citizens, Christian or not, might decide for themselves in the temporal sphere. Without this process of secularization, which separated the Church from the temporal power, there would have been no democracy, a system that is based on coexistence within diversity, civic and also religious pluralism, and laws that might not only not chime with Christian philosophy and morality but might indeed radically differ from them. The secularization of society was understood to demand, during the French Revolution, among the anarchist and communist groups during the Second Spanish Republic, for an important period of the Mexican Revolution and in the Russian and Chinese Revolutions, a frontal attack on religion in order to eradicate it from society. Monasteries and churches were burned down, people in religious orders and believers were killed, religious observance was banned, all forms of Christian teaching were outlawed and atheism and materialism were actively promoted. All this was not merely unjust and cruel but, above all, it was useless. The persecutions merely acted as a form of pruning because, after a time, beliefs and religious observance grew up again with renewed vigour.

Secularization cannot mean discrimination or a banning of beliefs and worship, but rather unrestricted freedom for citizens to practise and live their faith without any hindrance, as long as they respect the laws of their parliaments and democratic governments. And it is the obligation of these governments to guarantee that nobody should be subject to harassment or persecution for their beliefs and, at the same time, work in such a way that the laws are obeyed and are kept distinct from religious doctrine. This has happened in all democratic countries with issues such as divorce, abortion, birth control, homosexuality, gay marriage, euthanasia and the decriminalization of drugs. In general terms, the Church has limited its reaction to legitimate protests, such as manifestos, meetings, publications and campaigns to mobilize public opinion against the reforms and regulations it opposes, although there are also within the Church extremist institutions and clergymen who support the authoritarian practices of the extreme Right.

The preservation of secularism is fundamental to the survival and improvement of democracy. For confirmation of this point we only need look at societies where the process of secularization is non-existent or minimal, as in most Muslim countries. The identification of the state with Islam – the extreme cases are now Saudi Arabia and Iran – has been an insuperable obstacle to the democratization of society and it has contributed to maintaining dictatorial systems that impede the free coexistence of religions and exercise abusive and despotic control over the private life of their citizens, punishing them severely (with measures that can include imprisonment, torture and execution) if they stray from the prescriptions of the only authorized religion. The situation was not very different in Christian societies before secularization and it would have remained so if this process had not taken place. Catholicism and Protestantism reduced their intolerance and accepted coexistence with other religions, not because their doctrine was any less all-encompassing and intolerant than that of Islam, but because they were forced to change by circumstances: certain movements and social pressure put the Church on the defensive and made it adapt to democratic ways. It is not true that Islam is incompatible with the culture of freedom, no less so than Christianity. The difference is that in Christian societies, there was a process – propelled by nonconformist and rebellious political movements and a secular philosophy – that forced religion to privatize and step back from state control and, thanks to this democratic pressure, it prospered. In Turkey, thanks to Mustafa Kemal Atatürk, society went through a process of secularization (through violent means) and for some years now, despite the fact that most Turks are Muslim, society has been much more open to democracy than the other Muslim countries.

Secularism is not opposed to religion: it is opposed to religion becoming an obstacle to the exercise of freedom or a threat to the pluralism and diversity that defines an open society. In an open society, religion belongs to the private sphere and should not usurp the function of the state, which must remain secular precisely in order to avoid any monopoly in the religious sphere, for monopolies are always a source of abuse and corruption. The only way to demonstrate the impartiality that guarantees the right of all citizens to profess the religion they desire, or to reject all religion, is for the society to be secular, that is, not subordinated to any religious institution when carrying out its duties. When religion is kept to the private sphere, it is not a danger to democratic culture but rather it acts as a foundation and irreplaceable complement to this culture.

Here we get into a difficult and controversial issue about which there is no agreement among democrats, not even among liberals. So we need to tread through this terrain carefully, avoiding the landmines. While I am firmly convinced that secularism is indispensable in a truly free society, I also believe with equal certainty that for a society to be free it is necessary for there to be an intense spiritual life – which for the great majority means religious life – for, without it, not even the best-conceived laws and institutions function as well as they should and often fail or become corrupted. Democratic culture is not just built with institutions and laws that guarantee equity, equality before the law, equality of opportunity, free markets, an independent and fair judiciary (which means having honest and capable judges), political pluralism, freedom of the press, a strong civil society and human rights. There should also be a conviction among citizens that this system is the best possible, and a desire to make it work. This cannot become a reality without civic and moral values and paradigms deeply rooted in society, something that for the vast majority is indistinguishable from religious conviction. It is true that since the eighteenth and nineteenth centuries there have been in the Western world among the groups of free thinkers, exemplary citizens whose agnosticism or atheism was not an obstacle to their behaving irreproachably and honestly in the public arena, respecting the law and showing solidarity with their fellow men. This was true in Spain, in the first decades of the twentieth century, of many teachers who espoused anarchism. Their secular morality, with its strong social commitment, led them to become real social missionaries and, at great personal sacrifice, living spartan lives, they brought literacy and education to the poorest and most marginal sectors of society. One could mention many similar examples. But, with this proviso: it is the case that this secular morality could be found only in small groups. It is still an incontrovertible reality that, for the great majority, religion is the first and the main source of the moral and civic principles that buttress democratic culture. And, as is happening today in free societies in both the First and Third Worlds, when religion begins to fade, loses its dynamism and its legitimacy, and becomes superficial and frivolous – a mere social ornament – there may be tragic consequences for the functioning of democratic institutions.

The evisceration of spiritual life is happening in all strata of social life but it is in the economy that the effects are most visible.

The Catholic Church and capitalism never got on well. From the beginning of the Industrial Revolution in

Britain, various popes, in encyclicals and sermons, have railed against a system that, in their opinion, encouraged an appetite for material wealth, egotism and individualism, accentuated the economic and social differences between rich and poor and led people away from spiritual and religious life. There is an element of truth in these criticisms, but they become less persuasive if they are placed in a broader historical and social context: the positive transformations caused in society as a whole as a result of private property and a free economy, where companies and managers compete under clear and fair rules to satisfy the needs of consumers. Thanks to this system a great part of humanity was freed from what Karl Marx called the 'idiocy of rural life', medicine improved, and science in general progressed and living standards in open societies rose to historically unprecedented levels, while closed societies languished under a patrimonial and mercantilist regime that led to poverty, shortages and misery for the majority of the population and luxury and opulence for the elite. The free market, an unsurpassed and unbeatable system for the allocation of resources, saw the emergence of the middle class, which offered political stability and pragmatism to modern societies and has given the immense majority of citizens a decent life, something that had never happened before in the history of humanity.

Now it is true that this system of a free economy accentuates economic differences and encourages materialism, consumerism, the accumulation of wealth, and an aggressive, belligerent and egotistical attitude, which, if not kept in check in some way, can cause deep and traumatic upheavals in society. In fact, the recent international financial crisis, which sent shock waves through the West, was caused by the unbridled greed of bankers, investors and financiers who, blinded by short-term avarice, violated the rules of the market, deceived, swindled and brought about an economic catastrophe that has ruined millions of people throughout the world.

A further consequence of capitalism in creative, and what we might call 'impractical', endeavours, is that it causes a confusion between *price* and *value*, which is always detrimental to real value, and leads, over time, to the degradation of culture and the spirit that we witness in the civilization of the spectacle. The free market fixes the prices of products solely in terms of supply and demand, which has meant that almost everywhere, including in the most cultured societies, literary and artistic works of the highest worth are under-appreciated and marginalized because they are difficult and require a certain intellectual background and refined sensibility in order to be fully appreciated. By contrast, when the taste of the general public determines the value of a cultural product, it is inevitable that writers, thinkers and artists with mediocre or zero talent but who are very bright and flamboyant, who are skilled self-publicists or who know how to pander to the worst instincts of the public, achieve enormous success. The uncultured majority sees them as the best, and their works are eagerly sought after. In the field of painting, for example, as we have seen, this has meant that the works of real con artists have fetched staggering prices, thanks to prevailing fashions and the ways in which the taste of collectors is manipulated by galleries and critics. Such practices led thinkers such as Octavio Paz to condemn the market and argue that it has been the main culprit for the bankruptcy of culture in contemporary society. This is a vast and complex topic that would take us far beyond the subject of this chapter, which is the function of religion in contemporary culture. Suffice to say, however, that, alongside the market, there is another factor that has contributed to this anarchy and to the many misunderstandings that the conflation between price and value has caused in the worlds of arts and letters: the disappearance of elites, of proper criticism and of dedicated critics who once established aesthetic hierarchies and paradigms, a phenomenon that is not directly related to the market, but rather to an attempt to democratize culture and put it within reach of everyone.

All the great liberal thinkers, from John Stuart Mill to Karl Popper, including Adam Smith, Ludwig von Mises, Friedrich Hayek, Isaiah Berlin and Milton Friedman, argued that economic and political freedom achieved its full civilizing function, creating wealth and employment, defending individual sovereignty, the rule of law and human rights, only when the spiritual life of a society was intense and fostered a hierarchy of values respected and adhered to by that society. This was the best way, according to them, of doing away with or reducing the difference between price and value. The great failure, and the crises that the capitalist system faces again and again – corruption, the spoils system, mercantilist manoeuvres to gain wealth by infringing the law, the frenetic greed and fraudulent activities of bank and finance houses – are not due to inherent faults in the institutions of capitalism themselves but rather to the collapse of moral and religious values, which act as a curb that keeps capitalism within certain norms of honesty, respect for one's neighbour, and respect for the law. When this invisible but influential ethical structure collapses and disappears in many areas of society, above all among those that have the most responsibility in economic life, then anarchy spreads, bringing about an increasing lack of confidence in a system that seems to function only for the benefit of the most powerful (or the biggest tricksters) and against the interests of ordinary citizens who lack wealth and privilege. When religion becomes banal and disappears from many sectors of modern society – in particular among the elites – this helps bring about the 'crisis' of capitalism that we hear so much about, at the very moment when, with the break-up of the Soviet Union and the conversion of China into an authoritarian capitalist society, it seems that socialism, to all intents and purposes, has reached the end of its history. Frivolity morally *disarms* a sceptical culture. It undermines its values and introduces dishonest and, at times, openly criminal practices without any form of moral sanction.

And it is even worse if the person committing the crime – for example, invading the privacy of some famous person and exposing them in an embarrassing situation – is rewarded by media success and manages to enjoy those fifteen minutes of fame that Andy Warhol predicted for everyone in 1968. A very recent example of what I am talking about is the likeable Italian con man, Tommaso Debenedetti, who for a number of years published in Italian newspapers 'interviews' with writers, politicians, men of the cloth (including the pope) which were often reproduced in foreign newspapers. They were all false, completely invented. I was one of his 'interviewees'. He was found out by the US novelist Philip Roth, who could not recall any of the statements attributed to him by press agencies. He began to follow the news trail, which led him to the forger. Did anything happen to Tommaso Debenedetti for having deceived newspapers and readers with the seventy-nine false collaborations that have been unearthed to date? Far from being punished, the revelation of the fraud has turned him into a media hero, a daring and inoffensive trickster whose image and exploits have travelled the world, a hero of our times. And it is the case that, however depressing it might be to admit it, he really is a hero of our times. He excuses his behaviour with the nice paradox: 'I lied, but only to tell a truth.' What truth? That we live in fraudulent times, in which any offence, if it is amusing and entertains enough people, is forgiven.

Two issues have recently brought religion to the fore

and caused fierce debate in advanced democracies. The first is whether in state schools, funded by the public purse, all forms of religious instruction should be taken off the curriculum and become the exclusive preserve of the private sector. And the second is whether schools should ban girls and young people from wearing the veil, the burka and the hijab.

To ban entirely all forms of religious education in state schools would be to bring up the new generations with a deficient culture and deprive them of basic tools to understand their history, their tradition, and enjoy the art, literature and thought of the West. Western culture is imbued with religious ideas, beliefs, images, festivities and customs. To cut out this rich inheritance from the education of the new generations would be to deliver them, bound hand and foot, to the civilization of the spectacle, to frivolity, superficiality, ignorance, gossip and bad taste. A non-sectarian, objective and responsible education, which explains the hegemonic role of Christianity in the creation and evolution of the culture of the West, with all its divisions and secessions, its wars, its historical impact, its achievements, its excesses, its saints, its mystics, its martyrs, and the ways in which all this has had an influence, both good and bad, on history, philosophy, architecture, art and literature, is indispensable if we want to avoid culture degenerating at the rate that it is doing and having the world in the future divided between functional illiterates and ignorant and insensitive specialists.

The use of the veil or robes that cover a woman's body partly or entirely should not be the object of debate in a democratic society. Where is the freedom in all this? What sort of freedom is it that prevents a girl or young woman from dressing according to the dictates of her religion, or any way she wants? However, it is by no means certain that using a veil or a burka is a decision freely made by the girl, young woman, or woman who wears them. It is very likely that she is not wearing them out of choice, or personal freedom, but rather as a symbol of the condition that Islamic religion imposes on women, that is, their absolute subservience to their father or husband. In these conditions, the veil and the robe are not just articles of clothing, but emblems of the discrimination that women are still subjected to in Muslim societies. Should a democratic country, in the name of respect for beliefs and cultures, allow, in the heart of its community, institutions and customs (or rather prejudices and stigma) that democracy abolished centuries ago after great struggle and sacrifice? Freedom is tolerant, but cannot be so for people who deny it with their behaviour, deride it and, when all's said and done, seek to destroy it. In many cases, the use of religious symbols such as the burka and the hijab that Muslim girls wear to school are challenges to the freedom of women achieved in the West, which some wish to restrict, obtaining concessions and creating sovereign enclaves at the heart of open societies. Behind this apparently benign garb there lies an offensive that seeks to gain legitimacy for practices and behaviour at variance with the culture of freedom.

Immigration is essential for developed societies that wish to remain developed and, also, for this practical reason, they should seek out and welcome workers with different languages and beliefs. Of course, democratic governments should help these immigrant families preserve their religion and customs. But only on the condition that these customs do not weaken the principles and laws of democracy. And democracy does not allow discrimination or the subjugation of women to a servitude that negates their human rights. A Muslim family in a democratic society has the same obligation as any other family to adjust its behaviour to the laws in place even when these contradict customs and behaviour deeply rooted, in the case of immigrants, in their countries of origin.

This is the context in which we must always place the debate over the veil, the burka and the hijab. In this way we can better understand the decision of France – which is, in my opinion, just and democratic – to forbid categorically the use of the veil or any other form of religious uniform for girls in state schools.

THE SIGN OF THE CROSS

El País, Madrid, 27 August 1995
Translated by Natasha Wimmer

No one in Germany paid much attention to a suit brought

before the Federal Constitutional Court by two disciples of the humanist Rudolf Steiner from a remote village in Bavaria, alleging that their three small children had been 'traumatized' by being regularly obliged to see the spectacle of Christ on the cross on the walls of the public school they attended.

But every last family in the country knew – and a good many of them were left open-mouthed in astonishment to learn it – that the high court charged with ensuring that the principles of the constitution are justly upheld in the political, economic, and administrative life of Germany, and that admits no appeals, had found in favour of the plaintiffs. As announced by its president, the eminent jurist Johann Friedrich Henschel, the court's eight magistrates ruled that the Bavarian school's offer to replace the crucifixes on its walls with plain crosses – in the hopes that this simplification would 'detraumatize' the plaintiffs' children – was insufficient, and they ordered the state of Bavaria to remove all crosses and crucifixes from classrooms since 'the state must be neutral in religious matters'. The court then proceeded to stipulate that a school could keep the Christian symbol in its classrooms only by the unanimous agreement of parents, teachers and students. The shock waves from the scandal have reached even the peaceful lake in the Austrian woods where I've come seeking refuge from the heat of London. The state of Bavaria is not just a paradise of cholesterol and triglycerides, though the world's best beer and sausages may be had there. It is also a stronghold of political conservatism and a place where the Catholic Church is solidly rooted (I'm not suggesting that the one is related to the other): more than 90 per cent of the 850,000 Bavarian schoolchildren come from practising Catholic families. The Christian Social Union, the local variant and ally of Chancellor Helmut Kohl's Christian Democratic Party, exerts undisputed political control over the region. The leader of the CSU, Theo Waigel, was the first to protest the court's decision, in an article in the party organ, *Bayernkurier*. 'Because of the court's ostentatious efforts to protect minorities and progressively relegate the needs of the majority to a distant second place, our established values and constitutional patriotism are in jeopardy,' he wrote.

A measured response, if we compare it with that of His Excellency the Archbishop of Munich, Cardinal Friedrich Wetter, who was brought to the verge of apoplexy and – even more serious from the democratic point of view – civic mutiny by the affair. 'Not even the Nazis removed the crosses from our schools,' exclaimed Wetter. 'Are we going to allow a democratic state governed by the rule of law to do something even a dictatorship couldn't?' Of course not! The cardinal has urged civil disobedience – all schools must defy the court's ruling – and plans to convene an open-air service, on 23 September, that will surely attract the papal masses. The act will be celebrated to the belligerent eurythmics of a slogan coined by this same prince of the Church: 'The cross is here, and it's here to stay!'

If the poll takers have done their work well, a healthy majority of Germans support the rebellious cardinal Wetter: 58 per cent condemn the court's decision, and only 37 per cent approve of it. Seizing the moment, Chancellor Kohl has hurried to reprove the magistrates for a decision that seems 'contrary to our Christian tradition' and 'incomprehensible from the point of view of the content and the consequences that it may have'.

But perhaps even more damaging still for the cause that the Constitutional Court is championing is that the only politicians who have thus far come out in its defence have been that handful of shabby and vegetarian parliamentarians, lovers of chlorophyll and fasting – the Greens – whom nobody in this country of dedicated sausage and steak eaters takes very seriously. Werner Schulz, their parliamentary leader in Bonn, has proclaimed the state's duty to maintain a rigorous neutrality in religious affairs, 'especially now, when, because of the actions of Muslim fundamentalists and other sects, the freedom of worship is threatened'.

He has asked that the state stop collecting the tax that subsidizes the Church and that it replace the classes on Christianity taught in the state schools with teaching on ethics and beliefs in general, without privileging any specific religion.

From the refreshing cold waters of Lake Fuschl, I'd like to raise my hoarse voice in support of the Constitutional Court of Germany and applaud its clear-thinking judges for a ruling that, in my opinion, furthers the steady process of democratization that the country has been embarked on since the end of the Second World War, which is the single most important development in recent history in so far as the future of Western Europe is concerned. I say this not because I have the slightest aesthetic objection to crucifixes and crosses or because I harbour the slightest aversion for Christians and Catholics. On the contrary: although I'm not a believer, I'm convinced that a society cannot achieve a sophisticated democratic culture – in other words, it cannot be fully free or lawful – if it isn't profoundly suffused with spiritual and moral life, which, for the immense majority of human beings, is indissociable from religion. That is the opinion of Paul Johnson, who for at least twenty years has been documenting in his prolific studies the primordial role that faith and Christian religious practices played in the appearance of a democratic culture in the midst of the fog of arbitrariness and despotism in which the human race was stumbling.

But, unlike Paul Johnson, I'm also convinced that if the state doesn't preserve its secular character, and gives in, for example, to quantitative considerations such as those being brandished by the adversaries of the German Constitutional Court (why shouldn't the state be Christian if the great majority of its citizens are?), and identifies with a specific church, democracy is lost, in the short or the long term. Lost for one very simple reason: no church is democratic. All churches postulate a truth that is overwhelmingly backed up by the transcendence and wand-waving omnipotence of a divine being; against this omnipotence all rational arguments must dash themselves and be shattered. Churches would negate themselves – they would cease to exist – if they were flexible and tolerant and prepared to accept the basic principles of democratic life, such as pluralism, relativism, the coexistence of contradictory truths, the constant mutual concessions required to arrive at a social consensus. How long would Catholicism survive if, let us say, the dogma of the Immaculate Conception were put to the vote of believers?

The dogmatic and intransigent nature of religion becomes evident in the case of Islam, because the societies where Islam has put down roots have not undergone the secularization that, in the West, separated religion from the state and privatized it (made it an individual right rather than a public duty), obliging religion to adapt to its new circumstances or, rather, to confine itself to activities that were ever more private and less public. But it is supremely naive to conclude from this that if the Church were to recover the temporal powers it has lost in modern democratic societies, those societies would still be as free and open as they are now. I invite optimists like Paul Johnson, who believe such a thing, to have a look at those Third World societies where the Catholic Church still has the power to sway the making of laws and the government of society, and see what is happening there vis-à-vis film censorship, divorce and birth control, so that they understand that when Catholicism is in a position to impose its truths, it doesn't hesitate to do so any way it can, and not only on the faithful but also on all the non-believers within its reach.

That is why a democratic society, if it wants to continue as such, not only must guarantee freedom of worship and nourish in its bosom an intense religious life but also must take care that the Church – any church – not transgress the bounds of its proper sphere, which is the private. It must also be kept from infiltrating the state and imposing its particular convictions on the whole of society, something that can be done only by violating the freedom of non-believers. The presence of a cross or crucifix in a public school is as abusive towards those who aren't Christian as the imposition of the Islamic veil would be in a class where there are Christian and Buddhist children as well as Muslim ones, or the Jewish kippa in a Mormon seminary. Since there is no way to observe everyone's beliefs at once, the state's policy can only be neutrality. The judges of the Constitutional Court of Karlsruhe have done what they should, and their ruling does them honour.

A DEFENCE OF SECTS

El País, Madrid, 23 February 1997
Translated by Natasha Wimmer

In 1983 I attended a conference on the media in Cartagena, Colombia, presided over by the respected intellectuals Germán Arciniegas and Jacques Soustelle. There were at this conference, besides journalists from all over the world, some tireless young people endowed with the fixed and smouldering gaze of those who believe themselves to be in full possession of the truth. At a given moment, the Reverend Sun Myung Moon, head of the Unification Church, the organization that was sponsoring the congress through a front, made his appearance, causing a huge commotion among the youths. A little later, I realized that the progressive mafia had added to my roster of sins that of having sold out to a sinister sect, the Moonies.

Ever since I lost my faith, I've been in search of another to replace it, so I rushed with great excitement to see if the one espoused by that round and smiling Korean with his mangled English might be up to the task. This led me to read the magnificent book on the Unification Church by Eileen Barker, a professor at the London School of Economics, who has probably studied the phenomenon of the proliferation of religious sects at the end of the millennium more seriously and responsibly than anyone else (I met her at that conference in Cartagena). From her I learned, among many other things, that the Reverend Moon not only considers himself assigned by the Creator to the trifling task of uniting Judaism, Christianity and Buddhism in a single church but also believes himself to be a hypostasis of Buddha and Jesus Christ. This, naturally, utterly disqualifies me from joining his ranks: if, despite the excellent credentials that two thousand years of history have conferred on him, I am totally incapable of believing in the divinity of Christ, it would be hard for me to accept him in the form of a North Korean evangelist who couldn't even convince the US Internal Revenue Service (which sent him to jail for a year for tax evasion).

However, if the Moonies (and the sixteen hundred other religious groups and factions registered by INFORM, which is headed by Professor Barker) leave me sceptical, I feel the same way about those who for some time have devoted themselves to harassing these groups and petitioning governments to outlaw them, arguing that they corrupt youth, destabilize families, swindle their own members, and infiltrate state institutions. What is happening these days in Germany with the Church of Scientology gives this subject a troubling immediacy. The authorities of some states of the Federal Republic – Bavaria, especially – intend to exclude Scientologists from administrative posts, and they have organized boycotts of films featuring John Travolta and Tom Cruise because they belong to the Church of Scientology, and have banned Chick Corea from giving a concert in Baden-Württemberg for the same reason.

Although it is an absurd exaggeration to compare this harassment to the persecution suffered by the Jews under Nazism, as was done in a declaration signed by thirty-four Hollywood personalities in a paid advertisement in *The New York Times* protesting the German initiatives against Scientology, such acts do constitute a flagrant violation of the democratic principles of tolerance and pluralism and set a dangerous precedent. It's fine to accuse Tom Cruise and his beautiful wife, Nicole Kidman, of impoverished sensibilities and terrible literary taste if they prefer reading the scientific-theological productions of L. Ron Hubbard, who founded the Church of Scientology four decades ago, to the Gospels. But in a country whose constitution guarantees its citizens the right to believe in whatever they like, or not to believe in anything at all, why should the authorities feel that they may stick their noses into the matter?

The only serious argument for prohibiting or discriminating against religious sects lies outside the reach of democratic regimes; it is viable in those societies where religious power and political power are one and the same and where, as in Saudi Arabia or Sudan, the state determines which is the true religion, thereby assuming the right to prohibit false ones and to punish heretics, heterodoxy, sacrilege and enemies of the faith. In an open society, this isn't possible: the state must respect individual beliefs, as wild as they may seem, and must not identify itself with any church, since if it does it will inevitably end up riding roughshod over the beliefs (or lack of beliefs) of a large number of its citizens. We have seen this recently in Chile, one of the most modern states in Latin America but nevertheless little better than the Stone Age in some respects, since it still hasn't passed a divorce law, owing to the opposition of the influential Catholic Church.

The contentions wielded against sects are often correct. Their converts are frequently fanatics, their methods of proselytizing are intrusive (one Jehovah's Witness besieged me for a long year in Paris, trying to convince me to take the redemptive plunge and driving me into a frenzy of exasperation), and many of them literally empty their members' pockets. Couldn't one say exactly the same thing, though, about many extremely respectable offshoots of traditional religions? Are the ultra-Orthodox Jews of Mea She'arim in Jerusalem, who come out on Saturdays to stone cars driving through their neighbourhood, a model of flexibility? Is Opus Dei by any chance less demanding in the commitment it requires from its full-fledged members than the most intransigent evangelical operations? These are examples selected at random, out of many others, that prove many times over that all religions – from those validated by the patina of centuries and millennia, a rich literature, and the blood of martyrs, to the most incredibly flamboyant, based in Brooklyn, Salt Lake City, or Tokyo and promoted on the Internet – are potentially intolerant and by nature monopolistic and that the justifications for limiting or prohibiting the functioning of some of them are just as valid when applied to any other. In other words, one is left with two options: either all are prohibited without exception, as has been attempted by some naive regimes – the French Revolution, Lenin, Mao, Castro – or all are authorized, with the sole stipulation that they obey the law.

It hardly bears saying that I am a firm believer in this second option. And not just because the ability to practise a religion without facing discrimination or persecution is a basic human right. For the vast majority of human beings, religion is the only path leading to a spiritual life and an ethical conscience. Without religions there would be no such thing as human coexistence or respect for the law or any of the essential covenants that sustain civilized life. One very great mistake, repeated many times over in the course of history, has been the belief that knowledge, science and culture would eventually liberate man from the 'superstitions' of religion, until progress made religion obsolete. Secularization has not replaced our gods with the ideas, knowledge, or convictions that might have taken their place. It has left a spiritual void that human beings fill as best they can, sometimes with grotesque substitutes or multiple forms of neurosis or by heeding the call of those sects which, precisely because of their welcoming and tight-knit nature and their meticulous plan for all the instants of physical and spiritual life, offer balance and order to those who feel confused, lonely, or lost in today's world.

In this sense they are useful and should be not only respected but encouraged. Certainly not, however, with subsidies or taxpayers' money. The democratic state, which is and may be secular or neutral only in matters of religion, gives up that neutrality if it exempts one religion from paying taxes and allows it other privileges that are not extended to minority faiths by arguing that the majority or a considerable percentage of the country's citizens profess the same faith. This is a dangerous policy, because it discriminates in the subjective sphere of beliefs and promotes institutional corruption.

The furthest one should go in this regard is to do what Brazil did when it built Brasília, its new capital: donate a stretch of land along an ad hoc avenue and allow any church in the world to build a house of worship on it if it likes. Several dozen stand there, if my memory doesn't deceive me: big, ostentatious buildings, pluralistic and idiosyncratic in design, among which thunders, proud and bristling with cupolas and indecipherable symbols, the Rosicrucian Cathedral.

Final Thoughts

I end on a somewhat melancholic personal note. For some years, without me really noticing at the beginning, when I visited exhibitions, went to shows, saw certain films, plays, or television programmes, or read certain books, journals and newspapers, I was assailed by the uncomfortable feeling that someone was pulling my leg and that I had no means of defending myself against a developed and subtle conspiracy to make me feel uncultured or stupid.

Throughout all this a disturbing question was taking shape in my mind: why is it that the culture we inhabit has become so banal as to be, in many cases, a pale reflection of what our fathers and grandfathers understood by the term? It seems to me that this deterioration plunges us into an ever-increasing confusion, which might end up, in the short or the long term, in a world without aesthetic values, in which arts and letters – what we used to call the humanities – will have become little more than secondary forms of entertainment, unable to compete with the stimulants the large audio-visual media conglomerates offer the public, with very little impact on the life of society. This life, organized relentlessly by pragmatic considerations, would thus develop under the absolute control of specialists dedicated to the satisfaction of material needs and inspired by the pursuit of profit, the motor of the economy, the supreme value of society, the exclusive measure of success and failure and the *raison d'être* of individual lives.

This is not an Orwellian nightmare but a perfectly possible reality, which the most advanced nations of the planet, the Western liberal democracies, have been moving towards as the foundations of traditional culture have become increasingly degraded, being replaced by confidence tricksters who have led the general public away from genuine artistic and literary creativity, philosophical ideas, civic ideals and values, and that entire spiritual dimension previously called culture, which, although it was principally confined to an elite, in the past affected society at large, giving a sense to life that transcended mere material well-being. Never before have we lived in an age so rich in scientific knowledge and technological discoveries; never have we been better equipped to defeat illness, ignorance and poverty, and yet perhaps we have never been so confused about certain basic questions such as what are we doing on this lightless planet of ours, if mere survival is the sole aim that justifies life, if concepts such as spirit, ideals, pleasure, love, solidarity, art, creation, beauty, soul, transcendence still have meaning and, if so, what these meanings might be? The *raison d'être* of culture was to give an answer to these questions. Today it is exonerated from such responsibility, since we have turned it into something much more superficial and voluble: a form of entertainment or an esoteric and obscurantist game for self-regarding academics and intellectuals who turn their backs on society.

The idea of progress is deceptive. Of course, only the blind and fanatics would deny that an era in which human beings can journey to the planets, communicate instantaneously across the world thanks to the Internet, clone animals and humans, make weapons capable of blowing up the planet and progressively contaminate the air that we breathe, the water that we drink and the land that sustains us, has witnessed achievements unprecedented in history. At the same time, never has the survival of the species been less secure due to the risks of nuclear weapons, the bloody madness of religious fanaticism and the erosion of the environment. And perhaps never has there been, alongside the extraordinary opportunities and living conditions enjoyed by the privileged, such horrific poverty: hundreds of millions of human beings, in this prosperous world, still suffer, not just in the so-called Third World, but also in shameful enclaves in the heart of the most opulent cities on the planet. And not since the Great Depression has the world suffered from such financial crises and disasters, which in recent years have ruined so many businesses, people and even entire countries.

In the past, literature and the other arts were often the best way of attracting attention to such problems, providing a voice of conscience that prevented cultured people from turning their backs on the harsh and cruel reality of their times. Now, by contrast, it is a mechanism that allows us to ignore problematic issues, distracts us from serious concerns, and immerses us in a transitory 'artificial paradise', like a drag of marijuana or a snort of cocaine, that is, a brief vacation in unreality.

All these are complex topics outside the limited scope of this book. I mention them only as a personal impression of the crisis we are living through. In these pages such questions are inevitably refracted through the experience of someone who, since he discovered through books the adventure of the spirit, always held in high regard people who moved freely in the world of ideas and had clear aesthetic values that allowed them to have informed opinions as to what was original or imitative, revolutionary or routine, in literature, art, philosophy and music. Very conscious of the deficiencies in my intellectual formation, I have tried all my life to make up for these deficiencies by studying, reading, visiting museums and galleries, going to libraries, lectures and concerts. There was no sacrifice involved in all this, but rather the immense pleasure of discovering how my intellectual horizons were expanding, because to understand Nietzsche or Popper, read Homer, decipher Joyce's *Ulysses*, enjoy the poetry of Góngora, Baudelaire and T. S. Eliot, explore the universe of Goya, Rembrandt, Picasso, Mozart, Mahler, Bartók, Chekhov, O'Neill, Ibsen, or Brecht, enriched to an extraordinary degree my imagination, my desires and my sensibility.

Until the moment, that is, when I began to feel that many contemporary artists, thinkers and writers were pulling my leg. And that this was not an isolated event, something transitory, happening by chance, but a real process in which not just certain creators seemed complicit, but also their critics, editors, gallery owners, producers and a public of halfwits manipulated and conned by them.

The worst thing is that this phenomenon probably cannot be rectified because it already forms part of the way we are, the way we live, dream and believe in this day and age, and what I long for is just dust and ashes, with no hope of survival. But it might also be, since nothing can remain unchanged in the world we live in, that this phenomenon, the civilization of the spectacle, might also disappear without further ado, as a result of its own nothingness, and that something else will replace it, perhaps better, perhaps worse, in the society of the future. I confess that I have little curiosity for the future, about which I tend to be sceptical, given the way things are going. By contrast, I am very interested in the past and extremely interested in the present, which is incomprehensible without the past. Today there are, as I have pointed out, innumerable things that are better than in the lives of our ancestors: fewer dictatorships, more democracies, a freedom that encompasses more countries and people than ever before, prosperity and education that reach more people than previously and opportunities for a great number of people that never existed until now. But in the specific field of culture, with its volatile borders, we have gone backwards, without noticing or really intending to, and the deepest blame lies with the most cultured countries, which set out the guidelines and the goals that gradually influence the rest that follow their lead. And I also believe that one of the consequences of the frivolous corruption of cultural life will be that these great societies, in the long run, will be shown to have feet of clay and will lose their prominence and power because they will have squandered so lightly the secret weapon that made them what they became, this delicate substance that gives sense, content and an order to what we call civilization. Luckily, history is not a question of fate but a blank page on which with our own pen – our decisions and omissions – we will write the future. There is still time to put things right.

A final query, of universal relevance today: will paper books survive or will electronic books spell their demise? Will readers of the future just be using digital tablets? At the time of writing these lines, e-books have not yet taken over and in most countries paper books are still the most popular. But it cannot be denied that the move is towards e-books, to such an extent that it is not impossible to imagine a time in which readers of books on screen will be in the immense majority and the readers of paper books will be reduced to tiny minorities or will completely disappear.

Many people want the disappearance of the paper book and the triumph of digital reading devices to happen as soon as possible. Intellectuals such as Jorge Volpi, one of the main Latin American writers of the younger generation who has celebrated the arrival of the electronic book as 'a radical transformation of all the practices associated with reading and the transmission of knowledge', something that, he assures us, will give 'the greatest stimulus to the democratization of culture in modern times'. Volpi believes that because the digital book is cheaper than the paper book it will be more attractive and that imminently there will appear 'texts enriched not just by images, but with audio and video'. Bookshops, libraries, publishers, literary agents, proofreaders and distributors will disappear and all that will remain is a nostalgia for these archaic processes. This revolution, he says, will contribute in a decisive way to 'the greatest democratic expansion that culture has seen since . . . the invention of the printing press'.[1]

It is very possible that Volpi might be right, but this prospect, which makes him rejoice, fills me, and some others, including Vicente Molina Foix,[2] with anguish. Unlike Volpi, I do not think that the move from paper books to electronic books is harmless, a mere change in the 'wrapping', but that it will lead to a change in content as well. I have no means of proving this, but I suspect that when writers write virtual literature, they will not write in the same way as they have been doing until now, looking to have their writing materialize into that concrete, tactile and durable object that is the book. Something of

1 See his article 'Réquiem por el papel', *El País*, 15 October 2011.
2 See his reply to Volpi, 'El siglo XXV: una hipótesis de lectura', *El País*, 3 December 2011.

the immateriality of the electronic book will affect its content, as happens with the clumsy literature, without order or syntax, full of apocopes and jargon, sometimes undecipherable, that dominates the world of blogs, Twitter, Facebook and other Internet-based communication systems, as if the authors, by using this simulacrum that is the digital order to express themselves, feel free from all formal requirements, authorized to ride roughshod over grammar, synderesis, and the most elementary principles of linguistic correctness. Television is to date the best demonstration that the screen makes ideas banal and tends to turn everything it touches into a spectacle, in the most epidermal and ephemeral meaning of the term. My impression is that literature, philosophy, history, art criticism, to say nothing of poetry, all the manifestations of culture written for the Net, will doubtless be ever more entertaining, that is, more superficial and transient. If this is the case, new generations of readers will find it difficult to appreciate the worth and significance of demanding works of ideas or literature because they will seem to them as remote and eccentric as the medieval scholastic debates over angels or the alchemists' tracts on the philosopher's stone seem to us.

For Volpi, reading consists of mere reading, that is understanding the content of what is being read, and there is no doubt that very many readers share his views. But in the polemic by Vicente Molina Foix that his article provoked, Molina Foix reminded Volpi that for many readers, 'reading' is an operation that as well as registering the semantic content of the words also means savouring the beauty that, like the sounds of a beautiful symphony, the colours of an unusual picture, or the ideas of a shrewd argument, words united to their material form conjure up. For this kind of reader, reading is not only an intellectual operation but also a physical exercise, something that, as Molina Foix puts it well, 'adds an infallible sensual and sentimental component to the act of reading. The feel and the immanence of books are, for the amateur, variations on the eroticism of a crafted and cherished body, a way of loving.'

I find it difficult to imagine that electronic tablets, identical, anodyne, interchangeable, functional to the nth degree, can awaken the tactile, sensual pleasure that paper books awaken in certain readers. But it would not be strange that in an age that features the demise of eroticism, we would also lose that refined hedonism that enriched the spiritual pleasure of reading with the physical pleasure of paper's touch and caress.

MORE INFORMATION, LESS KNOWLEDGE

El País, Madrid, 31 July 2011

Nicholas Carr studied literature at Dartmouth College and at Harvard University and all the indications are that in his youth he was a voracious reader of good books. Then, as happened to all his generation, he discovered the computer, the Internet, the wonders of the great information revolution of our time, and not only has he spent a good part of his life making use of all the online services and navigating the Web morning and night; he also became a professional and an expert in the new communication technologies on which he has written extensively in prestigious journals in the United States and Britain.

One fine day he discovered that he had stopped being a good reader, and, almost, a reader at all. His concentration flagged after a page or two of a book and, above all if what he was reading was complicated and required a lot of attention and thought, he felt something tinkering with his brain, telling him to give up. This is how he puts it: 'I get fidgety, lose the thread, begin to look for something else to do. I feel like I'm always dragging my wayward brain back to the text. The deep reading that used to come naturally has become a struggle.'[3]

Concerned by this, he took a radical decision. At the end of 2007, he and his wife abandoned their ultramodern facilities in Boston and went to live in a cabin in the mountains of Colorado, where there was no mobile telephone and their Internet access came with a delay, was bad or non-existent. There, over two years, he wrote a polemical book that has made him famous. It is called *The Shallows: How the Internet Is Changing the Way We Think,*

3 Nicholas Carr, *The Shallows: How the Internet Is Changing the Way We Think, Read and Remember*, Atlantic Books, London, 2011, pp. 5–6.

Read and Remember. I have just read it at one sitting and it has left me fascinated, frightened and saddened.

Carr is not a computer drop-out. He has not become a contemporary Luddite anxious to do away with computers; nothing of the sort. In his book he recognizes the extraordinary contributions that services such as Google, Twitter, Facebook or Skype make to information and communication, the time that they save, the facility with which an immense number of people can share experiences, the benefits that all this can accrue to businesses, scientific research and the economic development of nations.

But this has a price and, in the final count, it is as great a transformation in our cultural life and in the way the human brain works as was the discovery of the printing press by Johannes Gutenberg in the fifteenth century, which allowed the reading of books to become widespread, whereas before it had been confined to an insignificant number of clergy, intellectuals and aristocrats. Carr's book is a vindication of the theories of the now-forgotten Marshall McLuhan, to whom nobody paid much attention when, more than fifty years ago, he argued that the medium is important not just for its content, but that the medium itself has a surreptitious bearing on this content and, in the long run, changes how we think and act. McLuhan was referring mainly to television, but Carr's argument, and the abundant experiments and accounts that he quotes in his support, shows how extraordinarily relevant this thesis is when applied to the world of the Internet.

The recalcitrant defenders of technology allege that it is a tool and that it serves the person who uses it and, of course, there are many experiments that seem to corroborate this, especially when investigations take place in an area where the benefits of this technology are undeniable: who could deny the near-miracle of an Internet user, in a few seconds, with a click of a mouse, being able to obtain information that, a few years back, would have required weeks or months in libraries or consulting experts? But there is also evidence that when a person's memory is not exercised because it relies on the infinite archive that a computer can offer, then it stiffens and weakens, like muscles that are no longer used.

It is not true that the Internet is just a tool. It is a thing that has become an extension of our own body, our own brain, which, also quietly and slowly, adapts to this new system of acquiring information and thinking, gradually giving up the functions that the Net can perform for it. It is not a poetic metaphor to say that this 'artificial intelligence' bribes and seduces our thought processes, gradually making them dependent on these tools and, in the final analysis, enslaving them completely. How can we keep the memory fresh and active if it is lodged in something that a systems programmer has called 'the best and largest library in the world'? And why should I try to keep my attention sharp if, by pressing the right keys, the memories that I need come to me, resurrected by these diligent machines?

It is not strange, therefore, that some Web fanatics

can state, like Professor Joe O'Shea, a philosopher at the University of Florida, that: 'Sitting down and going through a book from cover to cover doesn't make sense. It's not a good use of my time as I can get all the information I need faster through the Web. As soon as you are a "skilled hunter" online, then books are superfluous.' What is terrible about this statement is not the final phrase, but that this philosopher thinks that one reads books to 'get information'. This is one example of the havoc that this frantic addiction to the small screen can cause. And there's the moving confession of Dr Katherine Hoyle, a literature professor at Duke University: 'I can't get my students to read whole books any more.'[4]

It is not the fault of the students that they are now incapable of reading *War and Peace* or *Don Quixote*. Used to picking at information on their computers, without any need to concentrate in any sustained fashion, they have lost the habit and even the ability to concentrate and they have been conditioned to being satisfied by this flitting around to which the Net has accustomed them, with its infinite connections and leaps into complementary areas, so that they have become to some extent immunized against the sort of attention, reflection, patience and prolonged dedication to the text one is reading, and which is the only way to read great literature productively. But I do not think that it is just literature that the Internet is making superfluous: every form of free creation,

4 Carr, *The Shallows*, pp. 8–9.

not subordinated to pragmatic use, remains outside the type of knowledge and culture that the Web facilitates. Of course the Web can store Proust, Homer, Popper and Plato, but it would be difficult to imagine that their work will have many digital readers. Why take the time to read the books if in Google I can find simple, clear and approachable summaries of what they wrote in those dense, massive books that prehistoric readers once read?

The information revolution is far from being completed. Quite the contrary; in this field there are every day new possibilities and achievements and what seemed impossible is no longer so. Should we rejoice? If the type of culture that is replacing the old culture looks to us like progress, then yes. But we should be concerned if this progress leads to what an erudite scholar on the effects of the Internet on our brains and on our behaviour, Christof van Nimwegen, detected after one of his experiments: that to rely on computers for the solution to all cognitive problems reduces our brain's ability 'to build stable knowledge structures'.[5] In other words: the more intelligent our computer becomes, the more stupid we will become.

Perhaps there are exaggerations in Nicholas Carr's book, as always happens with arguments that defend controversial ideas. I lack the knowledge about neurology and computers to judge how reliable the scientific

5 Carr, *The Shallows*, p. 216.

tests and experiments that he describes in his book are. But it all seems rigorous and sensible, a warning that – let's not deceive ourselves – will not be heeded. What it means, if he is right, is that the robotization of humanity organized according to 'artificial intelligence' is now unstoppable. Unless of course a nuclear disaster, caused by a catastrophic accident or by a terrorist act, sends us back to the caves. We'd have to start again, then, and see if the second time round we can do it all better.

DINOSAURS IN DIFFICULT TIMES[6]

For many reasons I am moved to receive this Peace Prize awarded by German booksellers and publishers: for the significance it has in the cultural field, the distinguished intellectuals who have been its previous recipients, to whom I am now connected, and the recognition that it entails of a life dedicated to literature.

But the main reason, in my case, is its stubborn anachronism, its determination to understand literary work as a responsibility that is not limited just to the artistic sphere and is indissolubly linked to moral concerns and civic action. This idea of literature is what gave birth to my vocation; it has inspired to this day everything I have written and, at the same time, it is

---

6 Text completed in Paris on 18 September 1996 and read in the Paulskirche, Frankfurt, on 6 October 1996, in response to the award of the Friedenspreis (Peace Prize) given by the Börsenverein des Deutschen Buchhandels (German Publishers and Booksellers).

turning me, like the optimistic Friedenspreis, I fear, in this era of virtual reality, into a dinosaur in tie and trousers, surrounded by computers. I know that the statistics are on our side, that never as now have so many books been published and sold, and that, if the issue could be restricted to mere numbers, there would be nothing to fear. The problem comes when, dissatisfied with the comforting surveys on print runs and sales of books, which seem to guarantee the continuity of literature, we glimpse, as an incorrigible voyeur might do, what lies beneath the numerical veil.

What appears there is depressing. In our day and age, many books are written and published, but few people I meet – or hardly anyone, so as not to discriminate against the poor dinosaurs – believe that literature is much use at all other than as a means of alleviating boredom on the bus or on the underground, or as a means of providing raw material for television or film adaptations, and if the subject matter is Martians, horror stories, vampires or sadomasochistic crimes, then all the better. To survive, literature has become light, irresponsible and at times idiotic. That is why distinguished critics such as George Steiner believe that literature is already dead and why excellent novelists such as V. S. Naipaul proclaim that they will not write another novel because the genre now fills them with disgust.

But in this context of increasing pessimism about the power of literature to help readers better understand human complexity, be alert to historical realities and to resist the manipulation of the truth by the powers that be (that is why, when I began to write, there was a belief that literature meant something other than just entertainment), it is almost a relief to turn one's gaze towards the criminal gang that governs Nigeria, and murdered Ken Saro-Wiwa; those who persecuted Taslima Nasrin in Bangladesh; the Iranian imams who issued the fatwa condemning Salman Rushdie to death; the Islamic fundamentalists who have cut the throats of dozens of journalists, poets and dramatists in Algeria; those, in Cairo, who plunged the dagger that almost ended the life of Naguib Mahfuz, and regimes such as those in North Korea, Cuba, China, Vietnam, Burma and so many other places, with their censorship and their writers imprisoned or in exile.

It remains an instructive paradox that that while in countries that are considered the most cultured, that are also the most free and democratic, literature has become increasingly – this is a widespread conception – a trivial entertainment, in countries where freedom is restricted and where human rights are abused on a daily basis, literature is considered dangerous, a vehicle for subversive ideas, sowing the seeds of dissatisfaction and rebelliousness. Dramatists, novelists and poets in cultured and free countries who have become disillusioned with their craft because it seems to them to be succumbing to frivolity, or has already been defeated by audio-visual culture, should take a look at those vast areas of the world that are still not cultured or free. This might boost their spirits.

There literature cannot be dead, or completely useless; poetry, the novel and theatre cannot be innocuous, when despots, petty tyrants and fanatics are so fearful of them and are paying them the homage of censuring them and silencing or destroying their authors.

Let me hasten to add that, although I believe that literature should be engaged with the problems of its time and that writers should write with the conviction that, by writing, they can help others become more free, sensitive and lucid, I am far from advocating that the civic and moral 'commitment' of intellectuals will guarantee that they will make good decisions, support the best options to curb violence, reduce injustice and promote freedom. I have been wrong myself too many times, and I have seen too many writers that I admired also make mistakes, sometimes putting their talents to supporting ideological lies and state crimes, to delude myself. But I do firmly believe that, while remaining entertaining, literature must immerse itself in the life of the streets, in communal experiences, in history as it unfolds, as it did in its best moments, because, in this way, without arrogance or any pretence at omniscience, being brave enough to risk making mistakes, writers can offer a service to their contemporaries and save their craft from the dereliction that seems at times to threaten it. If literature is just about entertainment, having a good time, immersing ourselves in fantasy, free from the pettiness of everyday life, domestic hell or economic anguish, in a relaxed spiritual indolence, then literary fictions cannot compete with those supplied by our screens, be they big or small. Illusions forged by words demand the active participation of readers, an imaginative effort and, with respect to modern literature, complex feats of memory, association and creation, something that film and television images do not require of their viewers. And these viewers, partly as a result of this, become ever lazier, more resistant to entertainments that make intellectual demands on them. I say this without any hostile intent towards audio-visual media for I am a self-confessed film addict – I see two or three movies a week – and I also enjoy a good television programme (a rarity). But with this background I can say that that all the good films I have seen in my life, which amused me a great deal, did not even remotely help me to understand the labyrinth of human psychology as well as the novels of Dostoevsky, or the mechanisms of social life as well as Tolstoy's *War and Peace*, or the depths of misfortune and the exalted dignity that can exist in human beings as in the masterworks of Thomas Mann, Faulkner, Kafka, Joyce or Proust. Screen fictions are intense in their immediacy and ephemeral in terms of their effects: they seize us and then release us almost immediately; with literary fictions, we are prisoners for life. To say that the works of these authors are entertaining would be to do them a disservice, because although it is impossible not to read them spellbound, what is important about reading good novels always happens after the event; it is an effect that lights up in one's memory and over time. This fire is still alive within me because, without these books, for better or worse, I would not be who I am, I would not believe what I believe, nor would I have the doubts and certainties that sustain me.

These books changed me, moulded me, made me. And they are still changing and forming me, just as life is changing me. In them I learned that the world is badly made and that it will always be so – which does not mean that we should not do everything in our power not to make it worse than it is – that we are inferior to what we dream and live through fictions, and that there is a condition that we share, in this human comedy in which we are all actors, a condition that, despite all our diverse cultures, races and beliefs, makes us all equal and should also make us supportive of each other. That this is not the case, that despite sharing so many things with our fellow men and women, racial and religious prejudices still proliferate, along with aberrant nationalisms, intolerance and terrorism, is something that I can understand much better thanks to those books that kept me awake and on tenterhooks while I read them, because nothing sharpens our senses or makes us more alert to the roots of cruelty, evil and violence than good literature.

I can state for two reasons that if literature does not continue to play this role in the present as it did in the past – refusing to be merely light entertainment, becoming once again 'committed', trying to open people's eyes, through words and fantasy, to the reality that surrounds them – it will be more difficult to contain the outbreaks of wars, killings, genocides, ethnic conflict, religious struggles, refugee displacements and terrorism that threaten to proliferate, destroying the hopes for a peaceful world living together in democracy that were raised by the fall of the Berlin Wall. These hopes have so far been frustrated. The defeat of the collectivist utopia was a step forward, of course, but it has not brought about that universal consensus about living in democracy that Francis Fukuyama predicted. Rather, historical reality has become even more confused and complex and to make sense of it a good starting point might be the literary labyrinths imagined by Faulkner in the Yoknapatawpha saga and Hermann Hesse's *The Glass Bead Game*. Because history has become as disconcerting and evasive as a fantastic story by Jorge Luis Borges.

The first reason for literature's continuing moral importance is the urgent need to mobilize public opinion to demand that democratic governments take resolute action to support peace, wherever this might be breaking down and threatening to cause disasters, as in Bosnia, Chechnya, Afghanistan, Lebanon, Somalia, Rwanda, Liberia and so many other places where, right now, tortures and killings are taking place or weapons are being stockpiled for further killings. The paralysis with which the European Union witnessed the tragedy happening on its doorstep in the Balkans – two hundred thousand people dead and ethnic cleansing, which has, furthermore, been legitimated in the recent elections that confirmed in power the most nationalist parties – is dramatic proof of the need to shake public opinion out of its lethargic state of tacit acceptance or indifference and to rescue democratic societies from the civic paralysis that has been one of the unexpected consequences of the collapse of communism. Is it not the case that the dreadful crimes committed by nationalist and racist fanaticism in that powder keg – which has been dampened down but not completely extinguished – of former Yugoslavia, which could have been avoided by concerted action from Western countries, shows the need for a vigorous campaign in the field of ideas and public morality to tell people what is at stake and make them feel responsible? Writers can contribute to this task, as they did so often in the past, when they still believed that literature was not mere entertainment but also a way of raising concerns, sounding the alarm and guiding people to act for a good cause. The survival of the species and culture are a good cause. Opening people's eyes, expressing indignation in the face of injustice and crimes and demonstrating that there is room for hope in the most trying circumstances are all things that literature has known how to do, even if, at times, it has been mistaken in its targets and defended the indefensible.

The second reason is that the written word has today, at a time when many people think that the image and the screen will render it obsolete, the ability to delve deeper into problems, to go further in its description of social, political and moral reality and, in a word, to tell the truth far more effectively than any audio-visual medium. These media are much more constrained than books in their freedom of expression and creativity. This seems to me lamentable but incontrovertible: images on the screen are more enjoyable and entertaining but they are always superficial and frugal, often insufficient and very often inept, when it comes to telling, in the complexity of individual experience, what the courts ask of witnesses: 'the truth, the whole truth'. And for that reason their critical capacity is very limited.

I would like to pause a moment on this point, which might seem a contradiction in terms. The advances in technological communication have broken through borders and set up a global village where we all find ourselves existing together in the present moment, endlessly interconnected. We should congratulate ourselves on this fact, of course. The availability of information, of knowing what is happening on the other side of the world, of living it in images, of being at the heart of the news, has advanced far more rapidly than those great visionaries of the future, Jules Verne or H. G. Wells, could ever have envisaged. And yet, although we are very informed, we are more disconnected and removed than ever before with respect to what is happening in the world. Not 'distanced' in the way that Bertolt Brecht wanted his audiences to be: in order to inform their reason and rouse political and moral consciousness, to know the difference between what they saw on the stage and what was happening in the street. No. The fantastic sharpness and versatility with which the information media can transport us to the scenes of action across the five continents has turned television viewers into mere spectators and the world into a vast theatre or, better, into a movie, into an enormously entertaining reality show, where at one moment we are invaded by Martians, or we are presented with spicy gossip about personalities, and on other occasions we discover the collective graves of Bosnians killed in Srebrenica, or the wounded in the war in Afghanistan, missiles raining on Baghdad or children in Rwanda appearing with their skeletal bodies and their dying eyes. Audio-visual information, so fleeting, transient, striking and superficial, makes us see history as fiction, distancing us by concealing the causes and complexities of the events that are so vividly portrayed. This is a way of making us feel impotent to change that is occurring in front of our eyes on the screen, as happens when we watch a movie. It condemns us to passive acceptance, moral insensitivity and psychological inertia, as is the case with mass-consumption novels or TV programmes whose only purpose is to entertain.

It is a perfectly legitimate state to be in, of course, and it has its attractions: we all like to escape from objective reality into the arms of fantasy. This has also been, from the beginning, one of the functions of literature. But making the present unreal, changing real history into fiction, has the effect of demobilizing citizens, making them feel exempt from any civic responsibility, making them believe that they are powerless to intervene in a history whose script has already been written, acted and filmed in an irreversible way. Along this path we might slide into a world without citizens, only spectators, a world where, although democratic forms might exist, society has become the sort of lethargic society, full of passive men and women, that dictatorships seek to implant.

As well as turning information into fiction because of the nature of its language and the limitations of time at its disposal, audio-visual media find that their freedom to act is also constrained by the very high costs of production. This is not a predetermining but certainly an important factor that puts pressure on a producer's choice of subject matter and the ways in which a story can be told. The search for immediate success in not in this case a form of vanity or ambition: it is a prerequisite without which they cannot make a film (or the next film). But the stubborn conformity that is usually found in the typical products of the film and TV industries is not just the result of the need to reach the widest audience, aiming at the lowest common denominator to recoup the big budgets; it is also the case that since they are mass media, with an immediate impact on vast sectors of society, television primarily, but also cinema, are the media most controlled by the powers that be, even in more open societies. It is not that they are explicitly censored, although that can happen; rather they are scrutinized, advised, discouraged through laws, regulations, or political and economic pressure from tackling the most divisive issues. In other words they are encouraged merely to entertain.

This state of affairs has placed the written word and

its highest form of expression, literature, in a privileged situation. It has the opportunity, one might almost say the obligation, to be problematic, 'dangerous', as dictators and fanatics believe it to be, to stir things up, to be non-conformist, concerned, critical, to look for trouble. There is a vacuum to fill and the audio-visual media are not equipped or allowed to fill it with any great power or artistry. This work must be done if we do not want the most precious gift that we have, the culture of freedom and political democracy, to become degraded and eventually wither away, through the neglect of its beneficiaries.

Freedom is a precious gift, but no country and no people are guaranteed to enjoy it unless they embrace it, implement it and defend it. Literature, which lives and breathes thanks to freedom, and would be choked off without it, can help us understand that freedom is not a gift from heaven but a choice, a conviction, a practice and a set of ideas that must be constantly nurtured and tested. And that democracy is the best defence that has been invented against war, as Kant averred, something that is even more true today because almost all the wars across the world for at least a century have been waged between dictatorships or started by authoritarian and totalitarian regimes against democracies, while it is almost never the case – finding exceptions is like looking for needles in a haystack – of wars between two democratic countries. The lesson could not be more clear. The best way that free countries have to bring about a peaceful planet is by promoting democratic culture. In other words, by combatting despotic regimes whose very existence brings the threat of armed conflict, and the promotion and financing of international terrorism. For that reason I embrace Wole Soyinka's call for the governments of the developed world to apply economic and diplomatic sanctions against tyrannical governments that violate human rights, instead of supporting them or turning a blind eye when they perpetrate their crimes, with the excuse of safeguarding their investments and the expansion of their business interests. This attitude is both immoral and also impractical in the medium term. Because the safeguards offered by regimes that kill their dissidents, such as General Abacha in Nigeria, or the Chinese that have enslaved Tibet, or the military satraps in Burma, or the Cuban tropical gulag, are precarious and can disintegrate into anarchy or violence, as happened with the Soviet Union. The best guarantee for commerce, investment and the international economic order is the expansion of law and liberty throughout the world. There are people who say that sanctions are ineffective in promoting democracy. But did they not help to bring down dictatorships in South Africa, Chile and Haiti?

For writers to be 'committed' does not mean that they must abandon their imaginative adventures or their experiments with language, or the curiosity, bravery, and risk-taking that make intellectual work stimulating; nor should they turn their back on laughter or play because they feel that the desire to entertain is incompatible with civic responsibility. Great poems, plays, novels and essays have always entertained, enchanted and dazzled us. No ideas, characters or plots in literature can live and endure if they are not the result of bewitching magic tricks. 'Commitment' is not about abandoning aesthetic pleasure and invention.

It is about accepting the challenge that this end of millennium throws down to all of us and from which we men and women involved in culture cannot step aside: are we going to survive? The fall of the symbolic Berlin Wall has not made this question redundant. It has reformulated the question, adding unknown factors. Previously we wondered whether the great confrontation of the Cold War would turn hot and consume the world in the great holocaust of a single apocalyptic conflict between East and West. Now it is about knowing whether the death of civilization will be slower and more decentred, the result of a succession of many regional and national wars provoked by ideological, religious and ethnic factors, and by crude ambitions for power. The lethal arms are there and are still being manufactured. There are more than enough atomic and conventional weapons to wipe out several planets, along with our own small planet. The technology of destruction continues its dizzying progress and is even becoming easier to afford. Today a terrorist organization with few members and moderate resources has access to equipment much more powerful and destructive than anything available to the most barbarian predators such as Attila or Genghis Khan. This is not a fantasy problem on our TV screens. It is our problem. And if we all, including those of us who write, do not find an answer, then we could be faced, as in a movie, with the monsters of war escaping from their celluloid redoubt and blowing up the house where we thought we were safe.

During his years in exile in France, when the whole of Europe was falling under the seemingly irresistible advance of the Nazi armies, a writer born in Berlin, Walter Benjamin, devoted himself to studying the poetry of Charles Baudelaire. He wrote a book on the French poet, which he never completed, and he left a few chapters that we read today with a fascination that the most suggestive essays can inspire. Why Baudelaire? Why this topic at such a sombre moment? Reading him, we discover that *Les Fleurs du mal* contained answers to disturbing questions prompted by the development of urban culture, the situation of individuals and their spectres in mass and depersonalized societies caused by industrial growth, the forms that literature, art, dreams and human desires would adopt in this new society. The image of Walter Benjamin poring over Baudelaire, while the net that would end up choking him was tightening around him, is moving, as is the image of the philosopher Karl Popper who, at the same time, in exile on the other side of the world, in New Zealand, began to learn classical Greek and to study Plato as – these are his words – his personal contribution to the fight against totalitarianism. From this would come his seminal work, *The Open Society and its Enemies*.

Benjamin and Popper, the Marxist and the liberal, both

heterodox and original within larger currents of thought that they renewed and stimulated, are two examples of how, by writing, one can resist adversity, act and influence history. Models of committed writers, I cite them, in conclusion, as evidence that however rarified the air might become, and life might turn against them, dinosaurs can manage to survive and be useful in difficult times.

Acknowledgements

Although the limitations and errors that this essay might contain are mine alone, any possible good points owe much to the suggestions of three generous friends who read the manuscript and who I would like to thank: Verónica Ramírez Muro, Jorge Manzanilla and Carlos Granés.

Mario Vargas Llosa
Madrid, October 2011